ALSO BY JACOBO TIMERMAN

Prisoner Without a Name, Cell Without a Number

The Longest War

THE
LONGEST WAR
Israel in Lebanon

Jacobo Timerman

Translated from the Spanish by
Miguel Acoca

ALFRED A. KNOPF   NEW YORK 1982

Copyright © 1982 by African International Productions, N.V.

All rights reserved under International and Pan-American Copy-
right Conventions. Published in the United States by Alfred A.
Knopf, Inc., New York, and simultaneously in Canada by Random
House of Canada Limited, Toronto. Distributed by Random
House, Inc., New York.

Grateful acknowledgment is made for permission to reprint ex-
cerpts from the poems "To Israel" and "Israel 1969," from *In
Praise of Darkness* by Jorge Luis Borges, translated by Norman
Thomas di Giovanni. Copyright © 1969, 1970, 1971, 1972, 1973, 1974
by Emecé Editores, S.A., and Norman Thomas di Giovanni. Re-
printed by permission of the publisher, E. P. Dutton, Inc.

Library of Congress Cataloging in Publication Data
Timerman, Jacobo. The longest war, Israel in Lebanon.
Translation of: Diario de la guerra más larga.
1. Israel-Arab Border Conflicts, 1949–   —Lebanon.
2. Lebanon—History. 3. Israel—Politics and government.
I. Title.
DS119.8.L4T5513 1982   956'.04   82-48584
ISBN 0-394-53022-5
Manufactured in the United States of America
First Edition

This book is dedicated to Major Giora Harnik, of the Israeli Army. I never knew him. I know that he died at the head of his unit in hand-to-hand combat for Beaufort Castle in the first days of the Israeli invasion of Lebanon in what was the hardest battle of the war.

I know, too, that he was an active member of the Peace Now movement, and that he was against the war in which he killed and died.

I know that he was a pacifist.

I know that he could not live and die for his own ideas because he had to kill and die for the obsessions of inept rulers and vain military men who are running a nation created by moralists and dreamers.

I know that his mother, Raaya Harnik, is crushed with despair, and his friends are shattered.

I hope that this book will help us all. But I'm not so sure. We Israelis are confused and frightened.

Giora Harnik's mother wrote: "If we want to continue to be a humane, just, and incorruptible society, we must make sure that our sword is clean and drawn only in defense."

But Giora was already dead, and many more died after him.

The Longest War

1

General Ariel Sharon launched his offensive and began his war at eleven o'clock in the morning of Sunday, June 6, 1982. For me, the war had started sixteen hours earlier when my oldest son, Daniel, was called to serve. I drove to his house on Burla Street in Tel Aviv so I could accompany him to the staging area. Before setting off we stopped to pick up another member of his unit who lives nearby.

When it came time to say farewell to his family, my son and his wife went into the bedroom and remained there behind closed doors for two or three minutes. She is a third-generation kibbutz member, not used to the easy and spontaneous show of emotion of those of us of Latin origin. After two years in the same kibbutz, my own son blushes when my wife kisses him and when she nudges him to kiss his wife and two-year-old son yet one more time. He blushes even more when I get out of the car at his staging point, embrace him, and kiss him. His friend watches this with surprise, and his surprise deepens when I interrupt his farewell gesture to shake his hand.

Israelis are proud of their coolness in hard times. They are mistaken. They inflict on themselves an unnecessary burden that weighs heavily on their psyche, on their spiritual conflicts, on their morale. To grasp the full magnitude of their emotions, there is only one way: you must see them sing. See them more than hear them. They always sing. Alone on the streets they hum their songs. Everything that is born and grows here in Israel has a song: the triumphs as well as the defeats, the past and the future, a new crop in a distant colony in the Negev desert or a sunset seen from a hill that nobody has come to visit for pleasure in two thousand years. Each Saturday somewhere in the country neighbors gather together to sing. Each time they sing in a different place—on the grassy edge of a pond, on the haystacks of an agricultural community, or on the plaza of a small developing city.

Each Saturday the spectacle is shown on television. It is moving to watch those faces, particularly the old ones, when they close their eyes and, smiling, let themselves be carried away by the melody. The image I always had of old Jews was of lament and prayer. It is strange to see old men with unbuttoned shirts, bronzed by the sun, almost happy, I would say —if happiness can be attributed to the Israelis.

Shortly after I came to Israel in 1979, I was talking to the writer Amos Oz in Hulda, his kibbutz, and he asked about my plans. I replied that I wanted to be happy, something I had never known. He remarked that human beings do not need to be happy, nor can they be. Only an Israeli can say this with such ease, such coolness—and at the same time be young, beautiful, and struggling happily for the future. Exactly like Amos Oz.

In the army, there are hundreds of small groups who sing to the strumming of a guitar. At times a flute joins in. As a kind of extra touch, a popular television program shows these soldiers singing the songs of thirty, forty, or fifty years ago, the youthful faces of today with their long hair, some with beards, superimposed on other youthful faces, clean-shaven and with short hair, the very faces of those who created and inspired these tunes and lyrics.

Only when enraptured by their songs, drunk with them,

only then can you see Israelis relaxed, outgoing, sentimental, dreamers all. I would not, however, go so far as to say they are happy.

But the war really began the next day, when General Sharon unleashed his three armored columns. The Israelis don't actually feel they are in a war when the air force bombs Arab bases. All the planes always, almost always, come back. Only when the infantry takes part do they admit that they are at war. Not at once, of course, but every Israeli knows someone who has been called to arms. At first, it is always easier to think of an "operation." But after General Sharon was put in charge in August 1981, it became difficult to believe that he would be satisfied with anything less than a war.

After close and distant relatives have been mobilized, one is comforted by the new calls to duty. One believes that every soldier who goes to the front safeguards the lives of those already there. Perhaps this is why Israelis exchange news without making any comment. Such is the war in daily life. The florist's son was called up; he is a paratrooper. The florist knows that paratroopers are always on the front lines. The two sons of the delicatessen owner were called up. They are reservists, and perhaps won't go to the front. Also mobilized were the son and son-in-law of the dry-cleaner, a survivor of the Holocaust.

Many faces are missing. I cannot tell which ones they are, even though after living for three years in the Neve Avivim neighborhood I had seen them as part of the daily street scene.

Israelis allow themselves only two expressions. One of encouragement: "Everything will turn out all right," and another of solace: "It would be worse in Argentina," "In South Africa you'd have no future," or "In Turkey Jewish life is vanishing."

It was this way in all the previous wars. But now there is a sign of disquiet in the air, caused by the figure of Sharon.

Still, as the war begins, there are mixed emotions about the general, a certain ambivalence. Without him, perhaps, there might have been no war; but now that we are at war, it is best that Sharon, a great soldier, is in charge. We prefer no war at all, but it is better to win. Since there is no choice, the only possible activity is to listen to the news.

Sharon is everywhere. Around him, Israelis veer toward either pessimism or optimism, and wait more or less in anguish. In no other war has morale relied so much on each citizen's individual relationship with one single personality.

I can still see him at his command post on the southern front after the Six-Day War. It must have been in 1969, if I remember the date correctly. A mutual friend took me to visit Sharon at Beersheva headquarters. He was corpulent, imposing, but the figure in my memory bears no resemblance to the mass of flesh that he is today. In his office he stood before a huge map of the Sinai Peninsula and with a pointer he spent an hour explaining the campaign that had carried his troops to the Suez Canal in the west and to Sharm-al-Sheikh in the south. As he talked he became excited. My ignorance of military matters did not faze him, and he replied to each of my political questions in terms of military strategy. It appeared that for Sharon any political contradiction could be resolved with the proper military move.

Recalling that interview now, I think about the expression on his face as he pointed to stretches of territory and made predictions. It reflected more pleasure than passion, more sensuality than satisfaction, more dogma than talent. Still, how can he be denied talent, passion, and satisfaction? But I felt that the forces that moved him lay elsewhere, accessible only to him.

His relationship with military geography was almost lascivious. Napoleon would have loved him before a battle, supported him during the battle, but chopped off his head afterward. It is strange that a marshal of Bonaparte could have a career in a democratic army, in an army conceived by young socialist settlers in a state of strict constitutional controls.

Sharon's War had begun with Sharon. The war was pro-
jected, implicit, throughout his whole career. Perhaps it was
during that meeting in Beersheva that the war began for me.
I don't mean the invasion of Lebanon, only the premonition
that deep inside himself Sharon had reserved a war for Israel.

In the first months of 1982, we all knew that Sharon's War
would be an invasion of Lebanon. During this time there was
no political commentator, no important political leader, who
failed to discuss the pros and the cons in public. In addition
to a steady flow of news reports from Washington, Paris, and
London that counseled Israel to stay out of Lebanon, the
three former chiefs of staff of the Israeli Army who now sit
in the Knesset—Yitzhak Rabin, Haim Bar-Lev, and Mordechai Gur—expressed a certain fear and at different times
remarked that an invasion of Lebanon would not resolve the
Palestinian problem. There were no difficulties along the
northern border; the villages of Galilee were living quietly.

Why couldn't war be avoided? None of the rational explanations I have heard satisfies me. Yet I have reached a conclusion that doesn't settle the problem but at least helps me:
When an army is convinced of victory, its capacity for trans-
mitting this conviction is overwhelming. Nothing can stop it.
Even the most peaceful people are tempted by the possibility of winning. When you look into the faces of the mothers,
particularly those who lost sons in Sharon's War, the most
striking expression is one of astonishment. Death is always
astonishing; nevertheless, in war, it is inevitable. Perhaps the
astonishment is that one's own death—and the death of a son
is one's own—is inconceivable, unthinkable. And yet it is odd
that for a mother, even if she accepts the war in its fullest
meaning, the death of a son remains unthinkable.

All of us knew—especially Israelis and Palestinians—that
Sharon's War would be an invasion of Lebanon, and still the
only thing we could think of was that it would not be painful.
What else could we do? Some three months before the invasion, over lunch with Professor Michael Walzer at the Institute for Advanced Study, in Princeton, New Jersey, I sug-
gested to him that if the two of us decided to commit suicide

and explained in our wills that we were killing ourselves to stop Sharon's War, perhaps we could succeed in stopping it. In the lunar landscape of that snow-covered campus, above which rose a striking new glass building, all stone and beauty, I told him what I had seen in Israel, as we sought a way out, tried to plan some initiative.

But really, what could we do? The most privileged thinkers of Princeton and even of the entire United States, including some men of genius, would be more than ready to sign a declaration pleading for common sense and proposing solutions for the Middle East. Would this declaration be read and analyzed by General Sharon, by his aides, by his missile experts, his airmen, his sailors, and by his secret service and psychological warfare veterans? Would they pay attention to these men of Princeton who have written so many books and shared so many discoveries with mankind? Would they deem the declaration worthy of close study? Would General Sharon believe in the men of Princeton the way that Albert Einstein believed in them?

We cut pathetic and ridiculous figures, Michael Walzer and I, in our search for logic and sober judgment. Even if we had killed ourselves, would General Sharon have found in his heart the images of so many Jews who believed in moving the conscience of mankind by the generous surrender of their own lives?

On July 3, 1936, Stefan Lux, a Jewish film producer and journalist, killed himself at Geneva, the seat of the League of Nations. He wanted to call the world's attention to the plight of Jews in Germany, and he thought his suicide would shock mankind's conscience. He failed utterly, and his death did not trouble the delegates. The sessions went on; many people did not learn of what had happened until the next day. Nor did his death move his fellow journalists. This was evident from the short dispatches they filed and from the tiny space that newspapers devoted to the event. His gesture hardly moved the Jews for whom he had given his life. They were too busy convincing themselves that silence was the way to survival. Today exactly ten lines recall Stefan Lux in the *Encyclopedia Judaica*. And he did not save even ten Jews.

What would the world, or Israel, or General Sharon himself, have done with our two bodies? After that lunch in Princeton, life went on without change, yet I suppose that for me Sharon's War began that very day.

The opening of the war was not particularly hard. The first day we were dulled by the news, the second by the victories; the third we were certain that the operation could only last a few hours more. On the fourth day we tried to extract from the news and from conversations some indication of what was actually happening. Until that time, for us, the Israelis, the Lebanese children were not dead, their homes not reduced to rubble. Our consciences were clean, and did not have to assume any burdens.

Every Jew carries within him some old or recent scar from an inflicted humiliation. Heroism is a daily need, and in those first days it came in bundles. But afterward one had to decide whether those burning ruins of Lebanese cities had anything to do with heroism, or whether they were pictures of another war to demonstrate what Jews would be incapable of doing.

A man walks among those ruins, carrying in his arms a child of ten. A group of men, women, and children with their arms raised are under guard, and the expression on their faces, what their eyes say, is easily understood by almost any Jew. Yet we are forbidden to equate today's victims with yesterday's, for if this were permitted, the almost unavoidable conclusion would be that yesterday's crimes are today's.

It was around the fourth day that the guilt began. The war started officially on Sunday, June 6, and the guilt probably began unofficially on Thursday, June 10.

The first to understand the peril this entailed was Menachem Begin. In his numerous public appearances—almost daily, in fact—he strove to place Israel's attacks and raids within the vast context of military horror. If the Israelis had bombed Tyre, what about Coventry? If they had razed Sidon from the air and the sea, what about Dresden? If they had unleashed the full might of their firepower against badly organized and poorly equipped forces, what about the British in the Falklands? If some political leaders insisted on seeking a political settlement for the Middle East, why not invoke the ghost of Chamberlain and the ignominy of Munich?

Finally, if by chance the cautious Israeli television network let slip some footage and the screen showed a Lebanese child killed in a war in which (according to film shown in Israel) there are no victims, the prime minister did not lack the 1,500,000 Jewish children sent to the ovens by the Nazis, and, as a last resort, the pathetic memory of his own family.

Begin's critics believe he lapses into these absurdities because he lacks information, because he is ignorant of history. They assert that the comparisons are not apt, and that the new facts are used out of context. When we talk here, in low voices, the way one talks in a war, it seems to me that people don't yet want to acknowledge that Begin does not act like a statesman who plans his responses or like an irresponsible cynic. He is an intuitive politician who is ordinarily in perfect harmony with the mood of his natural audience: the Israeli voter.

A characteristic of Israel is that our postwar debates begin almost simultaneously with the first shots of the wars. Two weeks after the invasion of Lebanon, we are already deeply engulfed by the convulsions of one such debate. It is true that each of the "postwars" had its own characteristics, but they followed the same general pattern: the themes of controversy were the cost of the war, the skill of the war leadership, the political and military achievements, the economic recovery, the care of the wounded and the mutilated, the despair over the dead.

In the Lebanon war the familiar pattern was broken, and Begin perceived this at once. For the first time the Israelis were thinking about what they had done to another people.

They were feeling guilt, even shame. Never before had these reactions been seen among average men and women. Perhaps it can even be said that never before, at least in the last two thousand years, had the Jew had occasion to feel guilty and ashamed for collective damage inflicted on others. Throughout the Diaspora he was always the victim. His previous wars were in defense against aggression, and the acts of Jewish terrorism against Arabs were sporadic—the work of small groups who were rejected and disdained by almost all the population.

For the first time, war was not a response to provocation. Before, even in the worst of cases, it had been preventive. The understanding of this fact after only four days of fighting, when there were no doubts about the magnitude of the victory and the fears had vanished, was perhaps the first symptom of uneasiness that gripped some sectors of the country.

Israelis must be the most alert people in the world. Here wars can be unexpected but not unusual. They form part of what in Israel is called normality. Each detail of daily life, each gesture by a politician, each new word by an official is weighed, measured, and referred to the anxiety of the individual citizen. The fact that the invasion of Lebanon was the first war launched by the state of Israel could not go unnoticed.

There was no immediate negative outburst. Wars can also be launched for just causes and ample reasons. But for the first time some Israelis were arguing with themselves and discussing with others whether or not the cause was just.

It wasn't easy. All the conversations I had with Israelis other than leaders, experts, academics, fellow journalists, ended with commiserations and sorrowful consolation:

"How can I think of anything besides the three in my family who are in Lebanon? I want them back soon, so we need to win quickly. There isn't a family who doesn't have someone in the war. And you, Timerman?"

"My oldest son."

"Where?"

"He was called the first day. I went with him to the staging area. They were headed north."

"Now do you understand?"

But only a few days later the sensation of victory was total, the comfortable sensation of security inevitable. Emotions and intellectual concerns flowed spontaneously.

Israel is a country of interwoven remembrances. For each Ashkenazi (European) family the images of the bombed Lebanese cities were similar to what they had seen in Europe during World War II. That war in Europe was also alive in the minds of the Lebanese women waiting in line for water or for the distribution of food by military trucks, for the women and children searching the rubble of their shattered homes. Even the smiling Lebanese welcoming the columns of Israeli tanks brought back memories.

For each Sephardic family (most of them from Morocco) everything that was broadcast from Lebanon—the houses, the faces, the streets, the clothing—was an all-too-familiar sight. They could imagine those lives, their dramas, their penury, their reactions. Nothing was alien. Nothing brought back recollections of conflict. They had not been persecuted in Morocco or Tunisia. Even today they could go back to visit family that remained in those countries.

Israel is a small country. The population is small. All of us, absolutely all, learn quickly what happens to anyone else. On the tenth day of the invasion, small groups began to return from the front. A soldier receives a twenty-four-hour liberty pass. If he is stationed within Israel, even at an advanced frontier post, all he need do is stand on the side of a road and someone will pick him up. In two, three, or four hours at most, he will be home. If he is serving in Lebanon, a military vehicle will drop him at a border point, Rosh Hanikra or Metulla, and he is already in Israel and on his way home.

Among those first soldiers who returned, there was neither guilt nor shame. Still, I found them different from those on leave from other wars. They seemed stunned.

Veterans of the Six-Day and Yom Kippur wars knew that

the Israelis had always waged a clean fight. The rookies were aware of this because they had heard it from fathers who had fought in them or had studied them during military training. Now, for the first time, cities were being destroyed and masses of civilians had been killed.

They came back stricken with awe. They had seen it all, but did not know what it meant. When they talked about what they had witnessed, they seemed to be projecting a movie. But, strangely enough, they neither asked questions nor sought any meaning. A twenty-four-hour leave isn't much when six or eight hours are invested in the round trip. So many things wrapped in so much emotion are skimmed over quickly, and then they must return to the front.

But the civilians who remained at home after the visits of relatives and friends in the service began to feel the weight of these brief encounters with those who had been witnesses to something so strange.

While these first visits were taking place, there were other accounts. To be sure, they came from a more exclusive layer of the population. Some of the dozens of young Israeli reporters who had rushed into Lebanon—almost at the same time as the armored columns—came back. They had left their cars parked in Metulla, and drove from there to Tel Aviv, a two- to three-hour ride, or to Jerusalem, three to four hours away, the two cities where most journalists live and work. Some returned for twenty-four hours, others for forty-eight, and still others for good. But if they did not write about it or comment on radio and television, they brought with them something completely new: the smell of unburied bodies.

The odor of death itself is not new to the Israeli. Thousands of soldiers killed in the wars of the last thirty-five years rotted while awaiting burial. But the smell of women and children in streets and homes is different. The reporters said they could not get rid of it. And very soon at family reunions, at receptions, while waiting for the children to come out of the kindergartens, in the lines waiting their turn at the banks, the middle class of Israel started to discuss the smell.

They even began to make analogies, some of them totally outlandish. For instance, in the neighborhood around Tel Aviv University are some private clubs consisting each of a swimming pool, three or four tennis courts, a small green space, and a bar, and on Saturdays, naturally, they fill up. But flies swarm all over the clubs. Hanging from trees are special traps: large glass containers where the flies, attracted by a chemical, accumulate. The odor is unbearable. By the second Saturday of the invasion, the smell was called "the odor of Lebanon's dead." The cedars of Lebanon had been replaced by the dead of Lebanon.

The reporters brought back something else. Using binoculars from different vantage points, they had witnessed the systematic destruction of three great cities: Tyre, Sidon, and what was left of Damur after the civil war. This, too, was a first. Israeli Air Force bombs, along with artillery and navy barrages, were demolishing cities. The reporters had never seen such a thing before, never believed it possible; but they soon discovered it was the normal and natural result of a war in which you have an enormous military advantage.

They thought about it all, and theirs were the first thoughts that began to circulate among the Israeli people. Those who had not wanted to read or listen to the warnings about Lebanon from a small and isolated minority that had been overwhelmed by the collective euphoria now asked themselves whether it was possible that the Jews had done such things.

This seems a simplistic question for anybody who doesn't live in Israel. But here it is a painful problem. It erodes something invaluable if one is to survive—that is, the moral idea that Jews have of themselves.

The Israelis can put up with the notion that some of their soldiers are tempted by the opportunity for plunder that comes to a victorious army—and this subject was the beginning of reflections on the war, of discussion by small groups, of furtive glances between friends. They can accept the possibility that an individual soldier may be driven to acts of extreme violence. All the soldiers know the humiliation and torture that await them if they become prisoners of the Arabs. But never before had they transgressed certain moral limits.

In the postwar, however, it seems that day after day the moral edifice unstintingly maintained for thirty-four years of national independence is being undermined. It is true that the moral limits set in the Old Testament for this earth which devours its inhabitants do not respond to the ascetic vision of the prophets. But the suffering and oppression inflicted on the Jews in their Diaspora cannot be understood within a normal context—if the word "normal" has anything to do with all this.

With painstaking honesty, the Israelis have worked out the role of victim that the Jews fulfilled and continue to fulfill to this day in certain regions of the Diaspora. By necessity, this led to vindications and justifications. Then there is the weighty argument employed daily that allowances must be made for some emotional conditions when people go beyond accepted limits in their behavior toward others.

Yet despite this philosophical framework, which has served to maintain a certain mental balance, the Israelis never traded on the Jewish blood spilled in Europe. Strict moral limits were kept because, as a popular saying put it, "We cannot do to others what was done to us." There were also limits on hypocrisy. The use of the role of victim was prudent, almost humble, sober and dignified.

Many Israelis feel offended by the way in which the Holocaust is exploited in the Diaspora. They even feel ashamed that the Holocaust has become a civil religion for Jews in the United States. They respect the works of Alfred Kazin, Irving Howe, and Marie Syrkin. But of other writers, editors, historians, bureaucrats, and academics they say, using the word *Shoa*, which is the Hebrew for Holocaust: "There's no business like *Shoa* business."

This entire structure of moral principles and intellectual honesty is being battered by an argumentative process initiated by Menachem Begin and now being expanded at different levels.

The Israeli is proud of the efficiency of his army, of the courage of his soldiers, of the spirit of sacrifice of his officers. But he is careful in the use of epithets and bravado. He also knows that he has been fighting against an organization which—despite the vast arsenal of weapons at its disposal—did not have any true military experience and lacked planes and warships. The average soldier on his first leave was astonished to see how his heroism was being used when he himself had not yet digested the scenes of civil destruction he had helped to bring about in Lebanon. If such men came back already ashamed, this use of them provoked the first glimmers of guilt and unease.

Menachem Begin, assisted by his publicity machine, attempted from the beginning to expand the limits of the territory which the Israeli felt that he had the right to occupy as the historic victim of hatred and violence. But in these attempts the Israeli is finding still another confirmation that what he considered his rights as a victim have been stretched too far. With all this his identity has suffered a true shock, and now, out of necessity, he must rethink his very self. When Begin insists, as if it were a new discovery, that Israelis do not bow in silence when attacked, they understand this is not the change in their personality that the prime minister is broadcasting. After all, Israelis know they never once bowed to aggression in the one hundred years of active Jewish colonization of Israel. It is clear that Begin is actually announcing another kind of change, and it is then that they think of Lebanese women and children buried under the rubble of Tyre, Sidon, and Damur, and of the odor that clings to them. It is also clear that Israelis don't want to assume the new identity Begin is proposing. But they don't yet have a distinct idea of how to avoid it.

They throw themselves into drives for aid to Lebanon: chocolates for Lebanese children, clothing, building materials, fresh foods. As best they can, they channel their emotions into this endeavor until a new salvo of challenges surges from the ranks commanded by the prime minister: the Israelis are doing in Lebanon what the Czechs did not dare do in 1938, face up to Hitler's panzer divisions.

After such a pronouncement, lucid debate is a hard task. Slowly, in one conversation after another (and sometimes all Israel seems one huge chain of dialogues), we have to try to remember that moment forty-four years behind us. Only then does it become evident that the Palestinians in Lebanon had no panzer divisions, and that the columns of tanks were Israeli; that in 1938, England and France denied the Czechs the planes that the United States has so generously provided to Israel, along with communications systems, artillery, missiles, rifles, ammunition, the cannon on the Merkava tanks, and the broad diplomatic support. Would the Jews have fought if they had been abandoned like the Czechs? It's a painful question, and Israelis would have been happier if Begin had never raised it.

The Israeli knows that he is unbeatable in the Middle East. He doesn't fear for his security. He fears more for his moral health and mental balance, and this is why he needs peace in the region. He doesn't want to be forced to kill again in the way he killed civilians in Lebanon, and he doesn't want to think of when he must win the next war.

I walk in the park with my grandson and a neighbor asks me his age. "Two? Surely his turn will come with the '99 war."

It is precisely for the preservation of their moral health that Israelis hurl themselves into aid for Lebanon. It is possible that we will see a new phenomenon of collective solidarity, with Israeli volunteers working to rebuild Lebanon's cities. In the occupied West Bank territories, one already finds Israeli youths showing up weekly to work on the rebuilding of homes that have been blown up by order of the Defense Ministry. Usually these youths come from farming kibbutzim. One can even suppose that the reconstruction of

Lebanon could be accomplished faster than imagined because of the Israeli popular will to do so. Better, because of their need to do so.

Yes, the guilt had its beginning after the war was under way. For the first time an Israeli newspaper destroyed the myth that every victorious army wants to believe: that it is beloved by the people it has invaded. Avraham Rabinovich, a Jerusalem *Post* correspondent, wrote: "The Christians are undoubtedly happy the Israelis are there, but they will undoubtedly be even happier when they no longer have to be there."

In the first week of the war, Israeli television correspondents interviewing soldiers elicited descriptions of battles and greetings for the fighting men's families. But on the second Saturday a group of soldiers reacted with painful irony. They were shock troops and when asked how far they expected to advance, they replied: "Well, there's a vandalized synagogue in Ankara, so we will surely get there. Also there are Katyusha rockets in Moscow, so we will have to go to take them out." Another soldier interrupted: "Don't talk so much on television. Think of the dead boys."

And finally a nineteen-year-old soldier in the Golani Brigade, the famous and invincible Golani, remarked: "The war . . . what is war? . . . Only destruction and death."

Tomorrow I go to Lebanon. I still want to believe that we did right. All of us are at the front, not only Sharon. I still want to believe that it is not the war of a victorious general but of the entire people of Israel.

An army officer awaits me at Gesher Haziv, which lies on the Mediterranean near the Lebanese border. We will cross the border at the Rosh Hanikra post toward Tyre so that we can skirt the coast toward the north. If I can endure the smell of unburied bodies.

2

In this third week of the war, the heat has surpassed normal
levels. The summer has just begun, but Israeli faces show the
typical fatigue of August. Tel Aviv's beaches are jammed
with bathers—almost all Israelis. Tourists have vanished, and
we still don't know whether it is because of the war or because of the criticism of Israel, which is gaining massive expression in the countries of the usual visitors, the western
European nations and the United States.

The public swimming pools are also filled with bathers
because the school term has ended. But one can observe
these scenes of refreshing normality only by going in person
to the beaches and the pools. Israel's bathers do not appear
on television news, only those enjoying the Mediterranean
much further north, basking on the sands of the Bay of Juniye in the Christian sector north of Beirut.

Tel Aviv's bathers would be a negative example, proof that
the war effort and the sacrifice of the soldiers are not shared
by all Israelis. The bathers of Juniye are a positive example,
for they prove that the invasion has not caused any serious
trouble for decent, worthy Lebanese who proclaim their enthusiasm for the Israeli occupiers.

Soldiers, overwhelmed by the struggle, are shown on television. Also seen is the enormous energy invested in accompanying them, in helping them, in supporting their morale, and in maintaining their ties to distant families. And listed on the screen each day are the names of those killed in action, with their ages, their youthful ages.

But to realize that this war is not a common cause assumed by everyone in this country of solidarity, it is enough to go to the beaches and to submit to the riotous nightlife of Tel Aviv.

On television, the beautiful daughters of Lebanese bankers are sunbathing at Juniye, waiting for it all to pass, waiting for this minuscule incident to pass into Lebanon's history, just one more incident. But to see the razed cities, the deracinated lives, you've got to go there and look for yourself.

In either case, you must go to the streets. In Tel Aviv and Jerusalem. In Tyre and Sidon.

Is it possible that the human heart cannot stop beating and can endure, in a single day, the televised sunbathers of Juniye and the faces of Tyre's inhabitants going through their burned, destroyed, and disemboweled streets in the company of the armed official escort assigned to me by the Israeli Army? Yes, our hearts are doing it, and nobody has yet died of anguish. Also, every day we can see the Israeli dead, televised, and, back to back, Tel Aviv's bathers along the coast. It is not hard to perceive that our world is becoming a nightmare and that the conviction that this nightmare will not end is the only sense of security that we retain. For if the insanity should end, we would have to think and rethink the allowed images as well as the forbidden, and then perhaps our world would collapse.

It is Monday, the beginning of the fourth week of the war, and some forebodings are beginning to materialize and to fit the facts of reality.

The things that never should have happened in Israel have perhaps happened. The ideas that never should have been applied to Israel can perhaps be applied.

In the morning I received permission to visit Tyre and

Sidon, and assuredly I will absorb with intensity, like a good Israeli citizen, the fact that war brings inevitable destruction and that this one will serve to avoid even greater disasters. This very morning, the twenty-third of the war, the Jerusalem *Post*'s military correspondent, Hirsh Goodman, reports a dialogue, some recollections, and a pair of jokes from the front. These jokes make me recall other jokes that I did not want to believe until now.

Goodman writes: "Three Israeli military correspondents were surrounded by officers and men of four top fighting units, who accused them of covering up the truth, of lying to the public, of not reporting on the real mood at the front and of being lackeys of the defense minister. We were accused by the overwhelming majority of men—including senior officers —of allowing this war to grow out of all proportion to the original goals, by mindlessly repeating official explanations we all knew were false."

Israelis had painfully begun to understand that something unusual was happening, but never in the history of the state have the hypocrisy of a government and the cynicism of a high military chief been exposed with such clarity during wartime.

Many things were occurring for the first time. For the first time Israel had attacked a neighboring country without being attacked; for the first time it had mounted a screen of provocation to justify a war. For the first time Israel brought destruction to entire cities: Tyre, Sidon, Damur, Beirut. For the first time military spokesmen had lied. For the first time the Israeli press joined them in their successful mission of lying to the public. For the first time officers and men did not know the objective or the goals of the campaign. For the first time the actual damage inflicted on the invaded country was hidden along with the number of deaths. For the first time reservists on leave from the front demonstrated on the streets of Jerusalem because they consider themselves betrayed. For the first time jokes circulate openly.

An officer tells reporters, according to the Jerusalem *Post*, that the brigade's fool (that fool found in every unit) asked in which direction to aim the cannon, because every time we opened fire the army spokesman announced that the enemy had fired on us. Another joke, typical of an occupation army: An officer training soldiers to fire into the air when they have trouble with civilians warns, "but not into the air of their lungs."

For the first time it seems that an absurd situation, a sort of theater of the absurd, is being played out in the entire country, in the bosom of every group, in every family, and in every person.

During previous wars the questions were postponed. The wars were short. The questions did not challenge the permanent values of the state, which remained immutable and evidently unaffected. But Sharon's War is long, confused, and now for the first time questions are unsheathed during the fighting. For the first time they pose the possibility that the moral and institutional foundations of the state have been affected.

The long list of firsts is what has many of us jumping from one argument to the next, from one comparison to another, for we are trying to preserve something of our credibility, of our moral tradition, of our justifications, which were accepted from us because of our condition as victims of man, of nations, and of the world for an extended stretch of history. We are uneasy because in the fourth week of the war we cannot continue to deceive ourselves, and when we stop deceiving ourselves we begin to feel the shame—a strange and unreal sensation for a Jew, this conception of oneself as a victimizer.

In the Washington *Post*, columnist Richard Cohen enumerates the lies told in the past weeks by the Israeli government and its high officials. It's a good list. We should invite Cohen to Israel to help us reflect, instead of bringing in bureaucrats from dozens of foreign entities whom we manipulate and who in turn use us for their petty local projects. We Israeli journalists should have written Cohen's column, which argues: "Israel was a worthy cause. Its word meant something. Now that is less and less the case. Its moral standing has been eroded by its actions and its words. The invasion of Lebanon cost it dearly. What it won in territory it lost in credibility. It is no longer believed. Territory can't make up for that."

When certain critics accuse us of being Nazis, they do General Sharon a great service. Truly, we're not Nazis. But the accusation serves Sharon as a means of both discrediting the accusers and reclaiming his innocence. Yet we are not innocent. On this day that begins the fourth week of the war, when I am about to cross the border into Lebanon, we not only perceive that we have lost our innocence, we begin to have an idea of the magnitude of what we have done in the last three weeks.

I am in the dining room of Kibbutz Gesher Haziv on the Mediterranean, a few kilometers from the border. It is seven in the morning, I left Tel Aviv at five. It is a typical kibbutz mess, clean and neat, and the friendly attendants observe with interest and intelligence the dozens of journalists waiting to be taken to Lebanon by Israeli reserve officers.

The savor of old things remains. My generation was brought up with the conviction that the kibbutz and its way of life represent the moral tradition of the Jewish people as well as the political conscience that would lead them to become a normal people in a democratic state. Being in a kibbutz even for a few moments allows us to feel the umbilical cord that unites us with the pioneers who forged the nation. Today the death toll indicates that 20 per cent of the fallen in the war are youths from the kibbutzim, even though these settlements make up only 3 per cent of Israel's total population. A majority of these youths are against the war. But only when Prime Minister Begin and General Sharon decide to terminate the occupation of Lebanon and they can return to their kibbutzim will we know whether this is the last time that they have accepted military discipline without question, or whether Israeli youths will begin to use the strategy of the

U.S. movement against the Vietnam War. A great deal will depend on the political wisdom of the Palestinian leaders, on whether they abandon the strategy of rejection and the tactic of terrorism and adopt political means.

We're still living in total confusion and can't see clearly what we will do, how we will react. Giora Harnik's mother asks herself whether she did right to bring up her son in the spirit of patriotism that led him to obey General Sharon's orders blindly, and to die for them. Perhaps if she had taught him to hate the promoters of military magic, Giora would still be alive. The mother of another soldier asks herself whether she did right to instill pacifist convictions in him. He was assigned to the occupied territories, but he refused to serve in an occupation army. He spent two months in a military prison, then was let go and discharged. Afterward he found it impossible to start a normal life in a country where young men are required to present their military service record to obtain employment. He quit Israel and it's hardly possible he will return—rendered a wandering Jew because of a turn of history that the founding fathers did not foresee.

Still, in the hour that remains before we go into Lebanon to receive the official explanation of what we have done, I don't bother to make a list of the changes taking place in the country. I ponder the list of lies that Richard Cohen has uncovered for us and I toy with the idea of guessing those our escorts will tell us on this trip.

Each time I gaze on the fields of a kibbutz, I automatically think that in the past it was a desert. The fields of the kibbutz are beautiful, the gardens rich with flowers. The men and women who pass by radiate the possibility of a pleasant country, of an honest humankind. Yet what they show can't be true, and if it is indeed true, then it has neither power nor influence. How is it possible that this country—with its kibbutzim, political parties, pluralist press, active and distinguished academic life, with its parliamentary democracy—could not stop a war for which the preparations were known to all, for which the need was never demonstrated, for which the reasons were made up outside the context of reality by the feverish mind of a restless general?

Was this question the principal surprise, the pathetic innovation brought by this war to Israeli society? Here's a kind of confirmation: the defenses set up patiently and with great effort over so many years did not protect us from our internal madness because they kept us obsessed with the madness of others, of those outside. We believed ourselves indestructible because we were watching only the madmen outside our frontiers, and we remained defenseless against our own madmen.

Five months ago, on January 31, 1982, at a lunch in New York sponsored by Americans for a Progressive Israel, I remarked: "The founders of the Israeli Army called it the army for the defense of Israel. It is now an army for occupying foreign lands or to war against other nations." I had told the five hundred people there that General Sharon was preparing a war, and I asked, "Who's going to stop the crazy reactionary generals of our army?"

The officer who took me and two reporters to Tyre and Sidon was unaware of my New York speech; besides, he didn't even know who I was. But he knew his job as a reporter's escort. Congenially he led us through the rubble of two cities, though not for an instant did we come close to the human drama that had taken place. Two cities demolished in a painless and routine operation. Neither blood nor a bad taste in the mouth. We could look but it was impossible to see. To see we should have gone into the jails and hospitals, we should have talked to mothers seeking sons lost when the Israeli Air Force bombed open cities, cities without anti-aircraft defenses and without an air force, and we should have sifted through the rubble and touched carbonized bones.

Twice I tried. Going past a prisoner camp, I asked whether we could speak with the women who waited outside for hours in the hope of learning something and who weren't even sure that what they sought was there. (I remembered how my wife, my son Hector, and my rabbi went to police stations in Argentina to find a hint of my whereabouts.)

But to talk to prisoners or their families requires a permit. I don't have one and, of course, it must be applied for elsewhere.

I inquired whether I could walk alone in the marketplace. No, it was too dangerous, perhaps mines or an assault.

One last recourse remained. To look, to look and understand the meaning of what I observed, to understand and put to use all I had learned from reading and experience. War had burst into my life for the first time, as with my entire generation, with Erich Maria Remarque's *All Quiet on the Western Front,* which is about World War I, the Great War, as it was regarded in those days. Since then I don't believe I have been spared any of this century's horrors. Would this be enough to enable me to converse with the ruins of Tyre and Sidon and receive their silent testimony, which reached me in torrents, uncensored and ruthless?

In the implacable sun the blackened ruins smoked no more, but the dust and the wind welded them into a sticky mass. When an edifice is demolished, does someone remain imprisoned beneath that mound? I remained mesmerized before the rubble of this edifice that was Tyre. It is three weeks since our army was here. If anybody came in search of another, he is already gone. In these ruins there must be pianos, pots and pans, pictures of family members who went to America, school notebooks, hand-embroidered curtains, watches. Inside, underneath, must be daily routine.

If I could encompass all this in a single formula, it would be easier. A magic sentence that would say everything: "War is inexorable," "War is ruthless," "The war was unavoidable," or, "It was them or us." Yet resignation is impossible. Those of us who have been in Israel without running any risk and watching how General Sharon was preparing his war, the script as well as the dialectic, cannot accept the ruins of Tyre. Neither the explanations of stored weapons, nor the training camps, nor the terrorists who threatened us can justify this destruction. I try to follow the logic of my companions and compare danger against danger, threat against threat, death against death, and still I cannot understand why we have laid waste to Tyre. I even let myself go with the stream of their incredible arithmetic and I add the number of homes destroyed, remembering that since we passed the border into Lebanon I have not seen a single house that did not show some war damage. Remembering what I observed only three days before the outbreak of war traveling through Golan and northern Galilee, I add and subtract, I multiply and divide, and I compare; but still I cannot even arrive at anything that would give an Israeli citizen the right to be standing here, secure, protected by his own army and observing what his army has wrought.

The arithmetic is repugnant. The imagination is more generous; it allows a certain pity, a degree of confession, and, above all, it permits me to express my solidarity with those who once lived there. Belated and stupid, but that is all I have this dusty morning, June 29, 1982, as I attempt to re-create the awful human adventure that began here twenty-three days ago, as I defend myself from the statistics that pretend to prove beyond the shadow of a doubt that the crimes were inevitable, the assassins efficient, the madmen patriots, and the destroyers of Tyre humane.

Some buildings have crumbled, forming a kind of mountain. The bomb craters are still there. Other buildings have lost their innards and only their blackened walls remain standing. Still others are partially destroyed, and the remains are once again inhabited.

Upon arrival in Tyre our group expanded. Now we consist of two cars, five reporters, and two military escorts. A *Time* magazine photographer and a German reporter have joined us. Sometimes the escort is increased to five officers. I don't believe we run any risk, but they insist we do. I am not permitted to speak to people picked by chance, much less alone. I prefer not to talk to those they bring to me. When they insist, I converse with them in French, knowing that the escorts can speak only Arabic or English. Naturally it's impossible to have any sort of deep conversation. The escorts ask everybody to use English so that everybody can understand.

Those of us who have been in prison know how to speak with our eyes so that we can be understood when forced to talk in the presence of the guards. This is how I know that what a cordial and pleasant Lebanese is saying is contradicted by what I see expressed in his eyes. His English is clumsy, his phrases stereotyped. Whoever has been a prisoner or been forced to surrender knows how degrading this moment can be.

I understand the serene dignity of his gaze, and I recognize his proud personality. So I tell him what one prisoner tells another when they share oppressive circumstances: I wish him luck, lots of luck, and I ask him to have faith, lots of faith. I say this in a few French words, a signal of respect for his cultural tradition, and I hope that he understands I'm paying homage to his identity. Of course, I wish that I could tell him much more, but we prisoners know it is dangerous to compromise anyone who remains in custody. We know, too, that even listening can be dangerous. So I bow my head a little when I shake his hand: *"Adieu, mon cher monsieur."* I want to ask his forgiveness.

Yes, from some windows they greet us with shouts of *"Shalom"* in Hebrew. Passers-by also say *"Shalom."* The first time I reply. Perhaps they do it because every human being must adapt himself to circumstances. The rest is a vacuum, and the vacuum is permanent fear. Throughout the ages, how many times have people learned the language of the conquerors, imitated their gestures, and tried to divine their intentions, their moods? How many times must the Jews have done this? But I am not the occupier, and I can't stand it any longer. I don't respond to greetings. I don't fraternize with those I have subdued by force.

I recall in 1935 when the first news films of the Italian invasion of Ethiopia began to be shown in the movie houses of Buenos Aires. Then came those from Spain. Then came more and more war newsreels, and now I am here and I think I have never understood the meaning of war. Without talking to the victims, trying only to imagine how the dead were killed, one can make out the outlines of the terrifying abyss into which they were hurled.

This is what I try to do in Tyre and Sidon as I gaze on these ancient cities, reduced to ruins in a couple of weeks. There is no answer to my question, but the least I can do is to render them the homage of my anguish in the very same places where they suffered so much.

I regard the ruins and, summoning all I can remember about human beings, I try to imagine how they attempted to survive the night bright with fires. How were their tears and their cries? I look up at high windows that seem like empty eye sockets, and I try to conceive of the faces of the mothers as they hurled their children from burning homes—perhaps they ran down those now-vanished stairs, or did they cover themselves under blankets and mattresses? I try to think what I would have done if I had been in one of those burned-out rooms. I pick one, to one side, whose curtains miraculously remain, and I'm there with my family. We must decide quickly whether to flee together or break up, and how to break up, and where do we go.

The Chilean poet Pablo Neruda once visited Machu Picchu, the dead city in Peru. Walking through the silent stone streets, gazing through the dead windows into rooms in which nobody has lived for hundreds of years, he tried to imagine the intertwined lives of the vanished dwellers, their work and their loves. "Stone upon stone," he wrote. "Man, where was he?"

A building in ruins, the mountain of rubble that was once a building, the shattered street that was once littered with fruit peels, windows once gay with flowers, need their people. Among the ruins of Tyre and Sidon I needed a man so that I could reach a definite understanding. Not the man who had survived and was trying to adapt himself to the occupation, nor the one who kept, if only in his eyes, the keys to his humiliation and to his dignity. Walking through those ruins, I lacked the man who lived in them. I searched, like Neruda in Machu Picchu, for the dead man, the imprisoned man, the man who was still fleeing.

Everywhere shredded power lines dangle uselessly from posts. For three weeks there has been no electric power. But it is a clear morning in the Middle East, and in truth it's not illumination I seek. Yet the sight of those dangling cables repeating themselves endlessly produces such a picture of desolation and rupture that our escort interrupts the tour and drives us to the power company, where we are assured they are working hard to restore everything to normal.

These same magic words, "Everything is returning to normal," are repeated time and again during the seven hours we spend in Tyre and Sidon. That day the banks reopened. Proudly, we are taken to visit two. Soon there will be electricity; with electricity, there'll be running water. The fruit and vegetable markets are already back to normal. My escort tells me that Israeli merchants offered to reorganize them, but that the Lebanese showed they could do it themselves. He breaks into laughter when I tell him that throughout the world markets run smoothly because they are in the hands of the Mafia. Surely the Lebanese Mafia warned the Israeli Mafia that the war would really begin in earnest if they did not head back to Haifa and leave the Lebanese territory alone.

The escorts accept jokes in good humor. A joke or an ironic phrase now and then is all I permit myself so as not to accept in silence what they tell me. But my many years in journalism have taught me that an argument with a low-level functionary leads nowhere.

Only once did I lose control. We were commenting on the impressive display of Israeli military might. Camp after camp, supply and communications bases, engineering and information posts, field hospitals and columns of tanks moving endlessly along with mammoth artillery trucks. I ask: Can anyone in the Middle East oppose or present any opposition to the Israeli armed forces? Nobody, they reply. From a military viewpoint, we can seize all the Arab capitals.

If nobody can stop us, that means that nobody can threaten us. If Galilee was quiet up to a year ago when our air force bombed Beirut, I ask in simple and banal terms, in the least politicized way possible, what are we doing in Lebanon? If we have such a powerful army, why couldn't we do what we wanted without destroying cities and massacring thousands of civilians?

They aren't allowed to answer political questions. I don't persist. We return to the normality theme. But even when the cities are rebuilt, which will take many more years than to reopen a bank, a market, or a power plant, the return to normality is no easy task. It also means developing a culture, structuring a society. And even these do not fulfill the needs of normality, for the real prospect for Lebanon is that it will become a protectorate of Israel, which will control the ambitions and rivalries of Lebanon's armed factions and hold the country in the yoke of a *Pax Hebraica.* Even if the Palestine Liberation Organization, which started the 1975 war, is crushed, all the groups that have kept Lebanon in a state of civil war since 1958 remain. It makes no sense to blame everything on the PLO.

These are precisely the subjects that are impossible to talk about in Lebanon while on a visit guided by Israeli Army officers.

We return to Israel, to the border post at Rosh Hanikra, on a lovely mountain road skirting the Mediterranean, which rumbles below. The road is narrow and badly damaged by the intense military traffic.

My escort is relaxed. The visit went without any important incident. Those who deal with the foreign press are obsessed by the presumed conspiracy against Israel by the mass media. When a Norwegian photographer placed some Lebanese children atop some ruins in Tyre, my escort took a photo of them all so that later he could prove it was a staged picture. Yet the fact remains that Tyre is in ruins whether or not children walk on the rubble.

It all went off quietly. He is a reserve officer and his civilian life is ever present in his remarks. He tells us we must build a superhighway to replace the road we're traveling on, and that it could carry hundreds of thousands of Israeli tourists to Lebanon. Commerce will flourish.

I don't want to keep pricking him with my comments. Would Israelis actually go to Lebanon, where, even if the PLO is withdrawn, nearly 500,000 Palestinians will remain? Despite having occupied the West Bank for fifteen years, the Israelis can enter that territory only on armed patrol. How will commerce flourish? Galilee is becoming depopulated because nearly all development investments are going into West Bank businesses. What kind of normality can there be when 3,500,000 Jews are prepared to turn nearly 2,000,000 Palestinians into second-class citizens, with all the cultural, social, and economic degradation this means?

I return to my home in Tel Aviv, and do what all Israelis do after a trip. I telephone relatives and friends. At the beginning of the fourth week of the war, two questions are persistently repeated: How long will this last? Haven't we taken enough territory?

I recall one of the answers: We could not reveal the objectives of the invasion because we would have tipped off the enemy. Having seen in part how the Israeli Army seized in a few days all the territory it wanted to raze, I ask myself whether there really was an enemy barring the way; and whether in military terms he can really be called an enemy.

3

When I weigh the events of Sunday, July 4, the start of the second month of the war, I try to stand aside from the confusion created by the avalanche of contradictory news. I prefer to list developments that either surprise or please me, to see whether I can find in them the cogency I cannot find in official declarations.

Last night I took part in a meeting in Tel Aviv called by the Peace Now movement. We were 100,000 Israeli citizens ready to withdraw this very day from Lebanon and negotiate this very day with the Palestinians, regardless of who represents them, for the establishment of an independent sovereign state on the West Bank. Someone remarks that almost all of us there are Ashkenazis, only a few are Sephardic. I'm not impressed by the observation, nor do I feel guilty because the least socially and culturally developed sector of the population is against us and chants: "Begin, King of Israel." I have seen their counterparts in Argentina, solidly behind Perón even when the Leader was drowning them in alienation and in an economic crisis, creating the conditions for their repression by ensuing military dictatorships. The loyalty of these classes, always a majority, toward charismatic and seemingly invincible leaders guarantees neither the rationality nor the health of a political situation.

The poet Jorge Luis Borges, when he was persecuted by Peronists, used to say sarcastically that "democracy is the abuse of statistics." Naturally I don't agree, and perhaps not even Borges agrees with himself. But statistics are not devoid of morality and cannot ignore morality. It is entirely possible that the turnout of 100,000 Israelis under the banners of Peace Now will not modify the decisions of the Begin government, nor have much influence on developments. But it is proof of the upheaval and rejection provoked by the invasion in a significant sector of the Israeli people. It is also confirmation that the policy of General Sharon of turning the People's Army into a State Army will meet serious opposition.

I went to the meeting with my two-year-old grandson on my shoulders. Over the loudspeaker is read the message of a father whose son will not make him a grandfather because he fell in Lebanon a few days before a nephew fell in Sharon's War—only a few years after other relatives died in one of the other wars. How many years remain for me to try to stop the war that the State Army will send my grandson to fight?

Precisely because it is a Sunday, when the Begin cabinet usually meets, news is circulating through all the media. But, in general, the news is manipulated. I prefer to seize on one journalist's report which surely will have greater historical meaning. Yosef Goell points out in the Jerusalem *Post* that owing to military censorship and the policy followed by the Israel Broadcasting Authority, the Israeli public is not fully aware of the magnitude of the physical destruction of Lebanese cities and of the number of Lebanese and Palestinian civilian victims. He adds: "It is crucial that as a nation which has been involved in five wars with the Arab enemy and one that has realistic, even though regrettable prospects of engaging in a number of future wars, we come to grips with the moral questions raised by those casualties."

I don't believe I'm wrong in saying that 90 per cent of the debate in Israel over the war revolves around political or strategic issues. Yet it is depressing that a people which has

suffered so much does not start with moral considerations—
or, at least, that it does not start to consider immoral, if not
the war itself, then the coverup of the pain and destruction
that the war has inflicted on others. In the debates, the others
—those who have taken the different side—don't seem to
exist and, of course, have no relevance, at least on the question of the sufferings we are to blame for.

Some old-timers want to wait until the soldiers and officers
return from the war because there will be no censorship to
curtail their talk. It would be heartening if the soldiers par-
ticipated, for this would expand the base of support to the
process launched by the Peace Now rally in Tel Aviv's main
square, where the painter Yigal Tumarkin paraded with a
placard saying: "Arik [Sharon], Butcher of Lebanon; Arik,
Prince of Jordan; Arik, King of Israel." The defense minister
was shown crowned with a broom dripping red paint.

Maybe the return of the combatants will become a significant political event. Yosef Goell's commentary points out a
totally new phenomenon: "As the war in Lebanon approaches its second month, the growing division in public
opinion at home can no longer be hidden. The argument that
public criticism of the conduct of the war and of its rationale
should be muted as much as possible while men are dying at
the front is a powerful and valid one. But it is difficult to
sustain such an argument as time goes on.

"The corollary, that such criticism at home tends to under-
mine morale at the front, would be equally valid were it not
for the distinct impression that the criticism and uneasiness
that has surfaced this week were often the result of reports
brought back by soldiers returning home from the front on
their first leave.

"In a way, one could claim that the criticism and confusion
seeping back from the front are largely responsible for the
undermining of morale at home, rather than vice versa."

It is the first time that such a thing has occurred in Israel.
And it isn't happening without trouble. The charges of lack
of patriotism are broadcast carelessly, or wildly, by govern-

ment spokesmen. There is also the suggestion that every war is followed by a public debate in which the former soldiers participate, and that if today's debate is erupting before the war's end, it is because the war has been long, longer than usual. Considering the discipline of the Israeli soldier and citizen, this is difficult to believe. What is being felt on the home front, almost since the first day, is the magnitude and character of the deceit to which the country has been subjected. The people feel misled by what has been said about the bounds of its security, which is in fact greater than presented in official announcements. They also feel deceived because only now, in the course of the ongoing debate, are they becoming conscious of the political options concerning the Palestinian problem.

As for the soldier, he has simply concluded that he is engaged in a war different from that spelled out by his officers before he went into combat. It is impossible to find a similar event in the history of Israel. Beyond that, he is convinced that he has caused needless destruction of lives and cities.

Frustration interwoven with shame has gradually provoked in him a state of anger which, though it doesn't explode, prevents him from remaining totally silent. It is difficult to predict how many soldiers will ask the courts to prosecute their superior officers, thus repeating the incident in 1956 when four young battalion commanders (two of whom, Mordechai Gur and Rafael Eitan, later became army chiefs of staff) charged the commander of their units with wantonly sending youths to certain death. The chief they accused was Ariel Sharon. They also accused him of exceeding his orders and sacrificing troops without the possibility of gaining any military advantage. Only the leadership and authority of Moshe Dayan, and the pressure that he exerted to abort a court-martial, saved Sharon's career.

The Peace Now meeting, and what transpired in it, did not merit headlines in the media, but I believe it was an event expressing attitudes that will be of the greatest influence in our future development.

The statement by three Jews in Paris on the Lebanon invasion was buried in the Jerusalem *Post* in a dispatch on Arafat —in which the Palestinian terrorist leader refers to it. A curious way to report a statement issued by Pierre Mendès-France, an ex-prime minister of France; Philip Klutznick, former president of the Conference of Presidents of Major American Jewish Organizations, and Secretary of Commerce in the Carter administration; and Nahum Goldmann, a former president of both the World Zionist Organization and the World Jewish Congress.*

I sense that the attempt to hide their words from the Israeli people will boomerang against the Begin government. Public opinion is being subjected to a disinformation campaign, but it isn't badly informed, it isn't badly oriented. In two or three days the importance of the statement will be grasped.

Mendès-France, Goldmann, and Klutznick say:

Peace is not achieved between friends, but between enemies who have struggled and suffered. Our understanding of Jewish history and the imperatives of the moment lead us to affirm that the time has arrived for the reciprocal recognition of Israel and the Palestinian people. The sterile debate in which the Arab world questions the existence of Israel and Jews question the right to independence of the Palestinians must be ended. The real issue is not in knowing whether the Palestinians have this right, but how to accomplish it, while, at the same time, guaranteeing the security of Israel and the stability of the region. Concepts such as "autonomy" are not enough because they have already been used, more to avoid than to clarify. What is now essential is to find a political agreement between Israeli and Palestinian nationalism. Mutual recognition must be sought without delay. Negotiations must be started to accomplish the coexistence of the Israeli and Palestinian peoples on the basis of self-determination.

*Goldmann died in September 1982.

Amid the torrent of words that stuns us, perhaps so that we will stop thinking, this brief, terse, and moving statement sums up what it is possible to achieve on this very day to avoid more deaths and more destruction. I would add that its pursuit would help the Jewish people to regain their moral stature. It's not hard to imagine what it means to an Israeli citizen to realize the wisdom of this declaration of unity with our past underlined by "our understanding of Jewish history."

In Israel, people are intoxicated by slogans, repeated dozens of times daily, which strive to justify our actions by referring to our past sufferings. It is more than painful to hear how the Holocaust is being used to explain the invasion of Lebanon. One of the current jokes in Israel is that we have no more blood left in our veins because Begin has spilled it all in his speeches.

These three Jews in Paris were not carried away by military victory. Yet at the same time Begin remarks in a jocular tone that one of these days he'll visit Beirut. I believe the future of the Israeli and Palestinian peoples is spelled out better in the proposal of Mendès-France, Klutznick, and Goldmann than in Begin's omnipotent jests.

I note these things because they get to the heart of the matter. They will have a greater influence on our lives than the interminable negotiations to decide Beirut's fate—they and the letters that soldiers send from the front, the pressure they exert on their families. Almost all the letters that reach a kibbutz of Latin Americans of my generation speak of confusion, disquiet, and unhappiness—and they ask relatives to mobilize for putting an end to the war. Some letters, even petitions signed by groups of soldiers, reach the newspapers. The government is seeking legal means to punish those who do not share its idea of patriotism.

Thus we enter the second month of the war, and it is already more than evident that military success does not necessarily mean a political victory. One can already foresee that the outcome will be a great political defeat for Begin, which will find expression in a vast popular outpouring for a solution to the Palestinian problem. But we will have to wait until the drunken spree wears off and we do the accounting of what was gained in this war.

Even here in Israel, those who consider that all criticism of the government on the Palestinian issue weakens the Jewish people in general find solace in the conviction that now a political solution is inevitable. This way, at least, the evils unleashed by the invasion of Lebanon will not have been in vain.

It is possible that we are living through crucial moments in the Middle East's history. Yet for the cycle to end without more death and desolation, the two peoples who are playing out their destiny here must learn not to fool themselves and not to let themselves be fooled.

The Israeli people will fool themselves if they begin to believe—or let themselves be led to believe—that the political solution will be a result of the horrors produced by the invasion. Before the war there was already enough margin to work out a political solution. A lot of patience and honesty would have been required, but it was feasible. To say that every war has a positive aspect—in this case, a growing realization that in the Middle East there is no military solution —is an obscenity when one thinks of Lebanon's demolished cities, of the dead, of the mutilated; in brief, of the consequences we'll have to live with for years.

When in 1970 King Hussein massacred the Palestinians in Jordan, just as General Sharon is now doing in Lebanon, he thought that the Palestinian issue had been locked away for a long time. He was mistaken. It rebounded with greater force than ever, and, unhappily for the rest of us, the Palestinians still clung to their old errors. They were convinced there was a military solution to their plight. Both Israelis and Palestinians have paid a high price indeed for their belief in military solutions.

It is possible that the Palestinian people are only in an embryonic stage of their historical development and for this reason cannot achieve a political understanding of the Middle East. Unable to work out for themselves a relationship between their newly found identity and the regional context within which it must exist, they chose the easy way of terrorism. It was the simplest of ways: hijack a plane and celebrate the event as if it were the victory of Waterloo; seize an Israeli school, murder a few children, and announce it as if it were the sinking of the French fleet by Lord Nelson.

But this strategy of terror did not advance the Palestinian cause. It did not check the Israeli hard-liners; if anything, it strengthened them. Terrorist strategy failed in Argentina, Chile, Brazil, Spain, West Germany, Italy, and Uruguay even before the terrorists were savagely repressed. That the Palestinians have not drawn any sensible conclusions from their own experience, or that of others, is as much a failure of their allies as themselves.

The Harvard, Princeton, and Columbia professors who went along with them for years, were they allies or accomplices? Or were they simply vain and frivolous academics who wanted to prove a thesis? They institutionalized the political ignorance of the Palestinians, raising the PLO to the category of a national liberation movement despite its internal chaos, its lack of a coherent program, its terrorist practices, its stupid brutality, and its negation of history. They seized upon the idea of the historical inevitability of a Palestinian state, an idea shared by all progressive people. But the day, month, and year of the inevitable depended on the sacrifice of one, two, or three generations.

The principal task of the academics should have been to confront Palestinian terrorism with a clear and convincing picture of the political reality, not to save lives and property in Israel—whose existence they never quite accepted—but at least to save Palestinian lives. They preferred to feel important glorifying an obsolete and reactionary image, that of terrorist *machismo.* They seemed obsessed by their competition with academics who supported Israel, forgetting that in competing they risked nothing, not even their academic standing. But hiding from the Palestinian people the true relationship of forces in the region was a veritable act of suicide, conveniently, however, of other people. Had they worked with the moderates among the Palestinians and the Arab world within the bounds of a political strategy, had they understood—as it was their obligation to understand—that President Sadat was an ally, they could have forced the creation of a Palestinian state despite the obstructions of Israeli reactionary groups.

And now, betraying their duty as scholars, they resort to the magic of symbols that don't serve to mark a course, nor to instill guilt feelings in General Sharon, nor to alter the relationship of forces in the Middle East. To speak of a Palestinian genocide, of a Palestinian Holocaust, to compare Beirut with Stalingrad or with the Warsaw Ghetto, will move no one and will only serve to feed their egos and settle accounts with other academics in whom these images can arouse guilt feelings. Jews know what genocide is, a Holocaust, a Nazi.

We don't need, nobody needs, to resort to truculent comparisons to be desperate for the victims of Lebanon, for the homes destroyed, for the massacre committed by the Begin government.

All those who approached the Palestinians betrayed them. The democratic political leaders of western Europe led the PLO to feel that they formed part of the same institutional constellation, without warning them that the idea of a secular Palestinian state in which Jews would be a minority was simply the product of a dream, that history does not go back to such a point. When the western Europeans heard the PLO talk of a "Zionist Entity," they did not respond with an explanation of the meaning and power of Israel. They did not warn against dreaming of the liquidation of a state whose power these politicians knew only too well. They allowed the PLO to avoid the issue with ambivalent insinuations that not even the goodwill with which some of us in Israel heard them could convince us that they accepted anything less than the destruction of our country.

The French writer François Wahl has criticized the European left. In an article published in Paris the second week of the invasion, he said: "The European left, for its peace of mind, acts as if the Palestinians are ready to accept a state next to Israel; 'and if they have not yet announced it, it is because Israel itself does not recognize them.' Whoever frequents them knows only too well: this is untrue. Except in some instances, as a cover for propaganda needs, they have never accepted the Jewish state."

One of the wisest Palestinians, Elias Freij, mayor of Bethlehem on the West Bank, told a French newspaperwoman during President Mitterrand's visit last March that the PLO needed to recognize Israel at once, without any conditions whatsoever. The European politicians had the same information as Elias Freij, and greater experience. Why did they go along with the PLO's political babble? And if they did insist on strategy changes, how is it possible that they did not react to the PLO's ineffectual claims?

Each "political" triumph of the PLO marked by the establishment of a delegation in a Western country was actually one more push toward the abyss into which they fell. Each PLO diplomatic triumph in the UN was one more way of alienating the Palestinians from reality. The expression of "solidarity" by dozens of Third World countries was in reality, in its simplicity, a new ring of solitude around the Palestinians.

The Third World cannot help them. It can't help itself. It doesn't even exist. But the Palestinians were given top billing in the scenario that makes people believe in the Third World's power.

Twenty days after the invasion, the Arab foreign ministers held a summit meeting in Tunisia. The petition that the PLO presented its Arab League brothers had fourteen points. The Arab League was another betrayer of the Palestinians, giving them a sense of power and security. Yet it was clear that there were too many unresolved problems in the region, and the Palestinian sideshow allowed countries that needed to consolidate their position a chance to gain time.

The huge sums of money given to the PLO by some Arab countries inspired the belief that the Palestinians had an unlimited capacity to acquire weapons and ammunition. They brought joy to the arms industry, but none of their friends explained that with respect to the requirements of a modern war they were back in the Middle Ages; that Israel had reached a degree of military sophistication never before seen in the Middle East.

The Soviets recognized the imbalance of forces. They knew that the acquisition of weapons does not make an army, and even less so against Israel. They did not warn the Palestinians that their problem has no military solution, because for the Soviet Union Palestinian "rearmament" was its great Middle East opportunity.

The Soviet Union poured in surplus weapons, but there was no time to deploy them against a modern army. The Soviet military attachés in the Beirut Embassy kept their boss, Ambassador Alexander Soldatov, informed, but not the military commanders with whom they offered toasts for the triumph of the revolutionary forces.

And if any Palestinian leader had doubts, the Begin government came to the aid of the Soviet ploy. In his characteristically hysterical style, the Prime Minister did not let a week go by without denouncing the buildup of Palestinian offensive capacity. Every U.S. congressman who could be seized was taken to survey Israel's northern border, to be lectured on the route that the PLO's Soviet tanks would follow in their inevitable invasion of the defenseless Jewish nation.

The Palestinians could not escape this enormous trap, which was embellished with a revolutionary romanticism that had life only in the days of Mao's Long March or in Fidel Castro's Sierra Maestra. The Israelis charged that Beirut was the international center of terrorism, and the Palestinians believed that several hundred dropouts and neurotics and maladjusted imbeciles gathered from some twenty countries added up to a revolutionary vanguard that would lead the way to a bright future.

Why weigh the facts of reality soberly and why consider

the disadvantages of their own relative backwardness if more than one U.S. scholar considered it a privilege to review the world situation with Arafat? Why ask Indira Gandhi for the benefits of her political experience if Arafat was received in India with pomp? Why not believe in the value of the terrorist strategy if Arafat could address the UN like a chief of state, a resplendent gun at his waist?

Outside the window where I'm writing is a small military airfield on the edge of the Mediterranean. I know the significance of those helicopters that each minute head north or return from the north. They go to kill in Beirut or to bring back the wounded. They enrage me. So do the Palestinians, because they have been so stupid. Their innumerable friends, who have turned them into history's toys, also fill me with fury. And I'm angry, too, with us, with the Israelis, who by exploiting, oppressing, and victimizing the Palestinians have made the Jewish people lose their moral tradition, their proper place in history.

The Israelis . . . but who are we? We were also deceived about the nonexistent Palestinian military might. We were deceived about the danger to our cities and colonies in Galilee, where peace reigned for nearly a year until General Sharon broke the truce with the PLO.

Begin and Sharon delude us when they tell us we are trapped, that Israel is the Jew among nations, that nobody accepts us. They arouse in us the fear they need to make us obey orders and ask no questions. They have never told us of our real power, of our military capacity, of our battlefield superiority. They have terrorized us. When we finally discover our defensive possibilities, it is already too late to allow ourselves the luxury of a long political debate because we're involved in a war. We are as much deceived as the Palestinians.

When we're told that we're encircled, I ask myself if the contrary isn't true, if we are not the ones who have encircled our neighbors.

Each time that General Sharon cites statistics on the Israeli victims of terrorism, seeking our endorsement for his designs, he fills us with panic. Afterward, reporters are unable to confirm his numbers with any responsible source. Trying time and again to find a pretext to seize Beirut, he announces on television that 1,392 Israelis have been murdered by the terrorists. He warns us that even a minimal PLO presence in Lebanon is an invitation for more killings of Israelis. The prestigious journalist Hanna Semer, editor of the newspaper *Davar,* fails to reach this number even after adding up all the victims of the past fifteen years. But she cannot obtain a clarification from the Minister of Defense.

General Sharon needs our approbation or passivity for his grand geopolitical plans. He resorts to those magic formulas wielded by the military when they disdain civilian control of their actions, to those elixirs that cure everything but only if applied without answering any questions. We are deceived so that Sharon can put Lebanon under our protection, keeping the 500,000 Palestinians there as third-class citizens. Annex the West Bank, but let's hold enough Palestinians in Trans-Jordan for the needs of the Israeli construction industry and the sweeping of our streets. The South Africa of the Middle East.

Perhaps I'm mistaken. Sharon needs neither our approbation nor our passivity. He must keep the Israeli citizen in fear; he has accomplished it. He needs our fear; he has it.

Even in our country, they make the Jew live in fear.

4

In the fifth week of the war I went to a wedding at the synagogue on Ben Yehuda Street in Tel Aviv. Nobody speaks about the obvious: the small number of young men. Nobody asks why. Nobody mentions the war.

The fatalism of the Israelis is incredible—they accept whatever happens to them without asking themselves who brought it on them or why. Perhaps they will change with the invasion, and the psychological mechanism of passive acceptance will cease to work. If previous wars were events beyond discussion because we were driven to fight, this time we were shoved from behind. It is easier to question the one who gave us the shove (he is one of us and lives in our country) than those we must defeat on the battlefield. Nowadays Menachem Begin points out with some concern that for the first time in Israel's history open opposition and criticism are breaking out against a war while it is going on. It is becoming more and more evident that what Begin regards as a retreat from the national spirit is in effect a great leap toward the devising of a political answer to the problems of the Middle East.

Since the beginning of the war Menachem Begin has boasted of the consensus that his actions have found among the Israeli people and in the Jewish Diaspora. Even though this was never true, it is interesting that the prime minister himself finally acknowledged the falsity of this claim at a meeting with his party's parliamentarians in the fifth week of the war. Not only did he acknowledge this, he himself brought the subject up for discussion. Not one of his allies would have dared to raise the subject in front of Begin, for whom dissidence seems more a vice than an intellectual attitude.

It is possible that he is preparing for the postwar, when he will have to report the political achievements of the invasion. Without these, the military results won't matter much.

Begin is girding himself for a typical Israeli political debate in which accusations require no proof and weigh more than ideas or analysis. Surely he will charge Israeli opponents of the war with having foiled the final attack against Beirut and the final surrender of the PLO. Worried by the political activities of Egypt and Saudi Arabia, maneuvers he cannot defeat by force of arms, he will try to prove that the opposition solidified in the fourth and fifth weeks of the war, when the attack against Beirut was denounced in Israel as dangerous and self-defeating.

Israel is a country of great verbal violence. Anybody familiar with the history of Jewish institutions in the Diaspora knows the phrases of lament and of accusation that are the ingredients of the long civil war which has split the Jewish people for thousands of years. Amos Oz raised this notion of civil war ten days ago as we mutually commiserated in his kibbutz while talking about the war.

But it seems to me that more than verbal violence affects Israelis in their debates. It's almost verbal cannibalism. Words must, before demonstrating one's own judgment, eradicate the existence of the opponent, devour him.

On the twenty-ninth day of the war, Begin himself forecast the verbal cannibalism that would be loosed very soon, with the official start of the postwar. That same fifth week I had to ascertain whether all of us, myself included, did indeed exist before the war. We were struggling, we tried to resolve some problems, we hid from some contradictions. We were assaulted by nightmares, we loved, we lived other wars, and nothing ended in resolution. Everything was prolonged, postponed for future clarification. We lived with this prolongation as if it were a possible mutation, a time in which something would happen. Generally a war broke out. Perhaps because those delays ensured the inevitability of what should have been avoided.

When we are reminded of that time before the war, faces, promises, and incidents come back, and we become desolate. Yet we must accept that a war is neither the end of the world nor the beginning of another. It is sad, sad even for the dead.

In Israel there is no fleeing from time. Wherever you turn to escape the war, you'll run into a Jewish time. Something past, something present, something future. In the fifth week of the war, trying to flee my obsessions and even trying to flee from Israel, I met up with the Jewish boy who was orphaned and whom I bear within myself. It is as if the death of my father in Buenos Aires in 1935, and the dimension of Judaism that even here I have the need to understand and make understood, hold some message.

I was alone in the room, and in each room in that house lived a Jewish family. In the room were two beds; one for me, the other for my parents. There was also a table, three chairs, a dresser, and a radio. A neighbor who had a telephone told me to dress and go to the hospital, to the Jewish hospital, naturally, to see my father. She gave me an orange that I ate on my way to the subway station, throwing hunks of peel on the street. Along the 500 meters of Jewish streets I crossed, running in stretches, hopping from the curb to the street, stopping before shop windows. Some neighbors told me something, others looked at me and sighed. There wasn't much more: a word or a sigh.

For many years thereafter, I often reconstructed the half-hour that transpired from the moment the neighbor came into the room through the door that was always open because there was no window, and the moment I went down the steps of the subway station. From the first instant I accepted that my father was dead. I examined the meaning of every gesture I made while dressing, while accepting from the neighbor a coin for the subway ride; her looks, her strategies. The attempt to hide, the seizure of panic was—as I understood much later—part of my father's death. Afterward, in the hospital, came the fears. Fear of my father's body, which lay under a sheet in the large common ward, the bed shielded by a screen and sick people waiting patiently for everything to be over. Fear of my mother's despair, fear of the piety of relatives, fear of each face that came near in those days of wake, burial, and mourning. But everything would change, everything was already changing, and then I was afraid. Yet the anguish was in that first half-hour, born in those first moments when a father's death befell a boy of ten, changing his human condition abruptly and unexpectedly: his relationship with himself, the most painful of relationships and the most pathetic of changes. The fears were overcome, never the pain. I understood many years later; but I shall live with the pain for the rest of my life.

The Jewish welfare association that aided the poor provided me with clothing I had never possessed before, because my father had always refused assistance, wrapping his misery in a pride sustained by innumerable moral verses. I was entered in a Jewish club and paid no dues. I was taken on excursions and tours on Sundays. My mother and I received presents on Rosh Hashanah, Hanukkah, and Pesach, and she was helped to find work. The welfare people paid the installments still owed on the radio so we could keep it. Many years later I could reconstruct not only that first half-hour of pure pain, but the banal and naive gestures a boy of ten uses to hide his anguish; also the quick disappearance of the fears. I understood, too, why I never felt fear, never any fear, never among the Jews, and why among Jews I was filled with a sensation of well-being that often overcame my capacity to analyze words and actions that could and should have led me to rebel, why I was overcome by that lasting experience that was my first encounter with Jewish life, with that daily Jewish effort to survive and help others survive.

This spawned a conviction, surely false, that no Jew would lead another Jew to his death. Jewish solidarity dispelled my fears but not the pain. Yet Jewish solidarity includes neither pity nor love. Many times I thought that this attitude can only take root in peoples whose survival is not guaranteed by the mere act of existing. It's not a matter of being strong or weak, but simply that existence is not guaranteed, that it's not a normal and natural act. Without pity and without a father, I struggled with that death all I could; my human condition changed when I was only ten.

On one of the corners of the main street that divided the Jewish neighborhood, a man set up a shoeshine stand. He had features similar to my father's. I thought surely that my father had not died and that for the time being this was the only work he could find. My mother always complained that he never had any aptitude for getting suitable work. Several times a day I passed next to this father, or sat in a doorway to watch him work. I tried to figure out how much he earned a day and whether he had discovered a way to pass the money to me. At times I supposed that the Jewish solidarity —the clothing, the holiday cakes, the trips—were actually paid for by my father, now a shoeshine man. It bothered me that the shoeshine man had a mustache, although I understood that it was a necessity imposed by his situation. At times I saw some elegantly dressed man, not from the neighborhood, employ his services. More than once I thought I discerned in these elegant figures gestures very much like those of my father. I concluded it was more logical that my father had hidden his features but kept his gestures, which only I could recognize.

But these men dressed in clothes and shoes my father had never possessed aroused wrenching guilt feelings in me. Was I picking them out because they were clearly rich and my father only the shoeshine man? This pain was a constant in my life, and my father's death never left me. Much later I discovered that my father had just turned thirty-five when he died. It is true that since the day of his death I have known his age and repeated it whenever I was asked. But I never knew the significance of that age in the life of someone who is the father. When I searched for my father in the features and gestures of neighbors, teachers, taxi drivers, small businessmen, movie ticket vendors, and others, I always picked out old men, sometimes very old men.

I could never spell out the significance of the ages of fathers or the feeling age is supposed to awaken. As time passed, the thirty-five years of my father became the age of my older friends, then my age, then that of my younger friends, and then of my older son. But the pain remained inside me, immutable, even though my father had already become a friend and then a son.

There never was enough mercy to allow a return to my original life, the one I was born with, which had been changed with the death of my father, instilling in me a pain so physical that it was as if an arm had been added to me, or a sixth finger. Such was my life, making a theology out of culture and knowledge, but without the interminable questions, of the Jews. I was a boy who received used clothing from a Jewish welfare association, better than I had ever had, once at the beginning of summer and again at the start of winter, dividing the year into two semesters more important than the intervals imposed by the school year. I was a boy who was given pieces of cake on Jewish holidays, and excursions to enjoy the sun. The boarders in the Jewish orphanage had vacations, real vacations. In the summer they were consigned to the homes of pious Jews who lived in small cities throughout Argentina. My mother never placed me in the orphanage, but I envied these vacations and I paid close attention to neighborhood stories about orphans who had been adopted by very rich Jews. Even now, when I walk through great cities outside Israel, through neighborhoods where Jews live, I still seek my father. His grave is still open, and my pain is endless. I don't know what to do with him after so many years. Because my father was in love with his Judaism my pain is so Jewish, and because I carry inside me his Jewish grave, my heart has other open graves so that my father will not be alone. Inside of me I bear a Jewish grave-yard.

In the fifth week of war I'm not the only one trying to avoid the conflict. I know many actually do avoid it. One way is to accept a government trip abroad to explain the Israeli position. I remain here, shifting from one time to another, finding all the numerous Jewish codes, those used here, those that deal with security, survival, and the Holocaust. I flee to the countryside, and plunge through the narrow pathways of Lower Galilee. The flowers have already dried up, withered by the heat of summer. I stop on a hill, bending down to pick up some stones to throw. I can throw them and let them make circular ripples on the water—or at a planted field, or the desert. Anywhere I throw them, from atop a hill where I halt, in any of those different instances and different geographies, looking into the distance of a clear spring morning, or with eyes closed against the fierce noontime sun of summer, or in the company of a friend, or a son, trying to remember something, picking a place in the landscape, in the middle of a descriptive phrase, or reciting a poem inspired by a sudden romantic reaction, thinking of a dead man who was very close and very dear and whose grave is in the Jewish cemetery in Paris, going downhill by leaps and bounds or in small steps with the aid of a cane, touching with emotion some old stones whose meaning is inscrutable because I am dominated by ancient ignorance, seated at the bedside of a sick friend without understanding his mumbling, helping a child cross a street, lying on the ground under orange, apple, almond, olive, or fig trees on small squares of earth diligently worked, or between rocks on the sides of little round mountains, or on neat furrows in a dazzling valley, or after possessing and profoundly adoring a beloved body, my head resting on her bosom which is already breathing serenely, and afterward enjoying one's own fatigue. In any of these moments in Israel there is a weave mingling nostalgia, the past, remembrance, the future, the possibility that all will be destroyed, and it becomes clear, clearer than ever, that if survival is a necessity in the Diaspora, the only limit while waiting for Jewish history to complete its cycles, here in Israel it is not only a possibility but a real alternative.

I am seated on a bend of the road north of Haifa, and the road continues to the north. Now I'm standing on a stone esplanade by the sea, separated from the water by an asphalt road heavy with traffic, then green fields, and then the sea. I turn slowly to my left, toward the south, and below me, almost bordering the road, are the high stone arches of an ancient Roman aqueduct and also a stone amphitheater built some ten or twenty years ago. Still turning slowly, I see to my left the moving landscape of Galilee, extensive fields worked with particular care between mounds of stone that have been piled up, one by one, by the hands of Jewish farmers, and hills covered in many places with the color of flowers, especially red and yellow ones. I turn a little more and before me is the enormous building of the museum. It was designed with austere lines by the fighters of the ghettos in which the Nazis enclosed the Jews, and behind it are the homes, factories, stables, and gardens of the kibbutz that these same fighters, these few survivors of that epic guerrilla struggle, built for themselves after having fought still one or two more wars, or three, or four, and now in the same places where they are living. Still turning to the left, and, again on the other side of the road, on a hill across from the hill on which the kibbutz rises, I see the dusty olive green tents of a military camp surrounded by barbed wire.

This way I complete the sights that encircle me, and turn my eyes to the sea once more. The only thing I accomplish is an assault of reflections, of nostalgia, forebodings, and hopes. It distresses me to think I could fall victim to an abstraction right here, next to the sea.

Once again I turn around the same circle I have just covered, but this time I try to seek the hint of a meaning. I become aware that the circle is narrowing, everything is disappearing that in one way or another could have pleased me. There is no more sea, nor picturesque ruins, nor geography. Now I'm within a circle of three elements: the ghetto museum, the kibbutz of the survivors, and the soldiers.

I'm gripped by an increasing anguish. This need not be, because I could walk down to the road and let somebody take me away from this place. I could go toward the water's edge where the sun and the salt would exorcise ghosts and presentiments. Perhaps, as many times before, I could step below to an orange grove in the valley and lie on the fresh and sticky earth, rub soil on my face, nibble on an orange, and weep dolefully over so many troubles.

But I remain here on this stone esplanade, again repeating the circle from which I find no exit. I remain here, anguished, tired, leaning first on a wall and then with my back against that wall—and the circle has become so small I no longer need to look anywhere. I simply close my eyes, and there, within the circle, are the people, pressing against each other, next to each other, inside each other. There are the Jewish ghettos and the survivors in old photographs showing faces of unrecognizable biology, proud of their few stolen weapons; and the sons of the survivors in handsome uniforms with weapons dangling carelessly from their shoulders, confident of their strength and of the ease of their survival.

Sounds reach me from everywhere, dispersed, sometimes unidentifiable, sometimes unattainable. They are the only factor that keeps me in contact with things outside the circle. I remain seated, transfixed, gnawed at by the presence of those people who have so suddenly and surprisingly enclosed me, and enclosed themselves with me, or perhaps—and the thought stuns me—I have carried them inside and they have simply awakened from the lethargy into which I had plunged them so as not to suffer the weight of their meaning.

It could also be that earlier I could not endure them all together in that triple complementary presence, and that only now have I been imbued with a little more strength, an original and different strength.

The first sound I identify clearly, and which removes me from the circle, comes from the military camp. It could be mealtime, or the afternoon roll call. After that I am able to put things in a semblance of order and I seize the images represented by sounds, voices, noises. The children of the kibbutz leave the school in groups; perhaps the veterans are sleeping, without forgiving themselves even now for having destroyed their phantoms with this extraordinary display of beauty and vitality that surrounds us.

I pull myself together.

Groups begin to leave the museum—students, tourists, and soldiers. I start walking toward the parking lot. I remain alone while the others get on buses and trucks. Nobody appears completely sad, or completely happy, or completely silent about what he has seen in the museum, which I could not even enter because I was so smothered and enclosed in the circle.

I'm drenched in sweat, my clothes covered with dust, a bag dangling from my shoulder, weary. One hand, two hands reach out from the last truck, and they help me climb aboard. We're headed north. I sit on the truckbed amid a horizon of legs and boots and people seated with legs crossed, and I maintain the same silence as the others. The weariness that I share with the others, even though I have not been in the museum, won't leave me. It's possible they were especially tired, worn out, and overwhelmed by the permanent presence of the need or possibility of survival.

Thus we reach the frontier with Lebanon, that promontory above the sea called Rosh Hanikra, and it is hard for me to accept this place decked out for tourists, this rock which extends directly from the barbed-wire barricades at the border but which is laid out just like any promontory on the coast of Naples used to reach Capri, simply and innocently. We have come here directly from that museum of Nazi ghettos and still the water does not seem less blue than in Capri, and the tourists do not seem less German than in Capri.

It occurs to me that perhaps I've made a mistake, that only here is the circle completed, that the circle which had seemed so hermetic a few hours earlier is closing only now.

I behave like any other tourist. Just after I have complied with the requirements of visiting the restaurant hanging above the sea, of taking the cable car to the caves, of using the telescope to view the coast and the fields below (after waiting in line and putting a coin into the machine), of watching a naval boat leaving a wake in the sea and a military plane a white trail in the sky; after having completely joined in the ceremony of the tourists to the rear of that military post on the border, between barbed-wire barricades; only then do I seem able to dwell on the most intimate secrets and questions.

I discover I am also ready for the other landscapes, made up of the faces of the people who belong to those barbed-wire barricades and those roads; and when I achieve the beginning of this identification with them, I understand I am approaching my own identity.

Now I am convinced that the circle will not strangle me. Moreover, that it's not even a circle, that there won't even be four characters. Identity is directly linked with survival, it assures it. I repeat this sentence several times. Identity assures survival. Identity is survival.

An agnostic savoring the taste of a newly created fetish.

I enjoy moments of true peace, looking at the sea and repeating the sentence as if it were a test. Perhaps I am testing the other, the one I was for so many years. Perhaps, at last, I am a Jew capable of creating a remembrance unencumbered by nostalgia.

And now I see how the dawns break in this country, the sun always appearing behind some hill. And as I have seen many dawns, I think of the many nightfalls in this country where every evening the sun falls into the sea.

It didn't seem proper to allow myself to be tempted by nature, as I would have done in other times, and just remain in the landscape for days and days and days. But I couldn't avoid it.

Even though every moment my yesterday, all my yesterdays, are tested, confronted with several possible futures, Israel's nature imposes its presence upon me. More than nature, I would say it is geography.

The small country can be seen in little time, and it can be distinguished and encompassed in brief intervals. Each one of these minuscule intervals modifies the spectacle offered. All this gives one's relationship with the geography a personal, an intimate character.

It's a geography of humanistic content to which one can resort and, at the same time, make a participant in everyone's life. The way that the person to whom one confesses or laments participates in the life of another; in silence.

I couldn't say that I feel entrapped by the geography. I slide through it and embrace its warm camaraderie. I remain alone with the geography of Israel, pursuing the ways of its contradictory roads, and at no time do I experience the challenge of those majestic encounters with nature that have arisen before me in so many countries and continents.

There is intimacy in this geography.

I remain apart from the inhabitants, devoted only to the geography, and again I sense the beautiful fellowship of youth, but without demands and disquiet.

It's a cordial geography that invites friendship. Roadways, rains or flowers, deserts or stars establish a pleasant, amiable complicity with man.

It has made innumerable friends in the country, and watching their faces as they travel through it, I feel them conscious of their friendship with the geography. It can overcome all their demands. They display no anxiety, no frustration.

I've sat among them, not quite next to them, somewhat aloof, during nights in the open air, letting myself be enveloped more by the sounds of their voices than by the words or lyrics of their songs, and I discovered that in Israel the geography allowed those people to become a part of me.

It is reassuring to become part of this geography of small places. A geography that, as days and nights pass, changes into an unusual and mysterious invitation to familiarity and ownership, into unequivocal acceptance.

After so many laborious discussions on the character of the country, on its reality, its destiny, after suffering so many tribulations over the heart of the matter, my discovery of the geography was intensely moving.

I stayed attached to the novelty of being entwined with a geography in which history forms only a part. Now I understood how this geography makes itself felt in the great ideological and religious adventure that has unfolded in this country in the course of the century. Surveying this geography which transcends nature, I realized how my identity expanded with ease—without tricks or fears, without deceptions or parables.

There were months of trips, with brief interruptions. The short distances required meditation the same day while watching the sea or the mountain or the planted valleys. It was impossible to go from one mood to the next, from one reflection to another. But I absorbed the landscape comfortably, easily. I began to discover that this geography has its own internal story, an intimate causality that weaves one landscape with the next.

Time after time I was tempted to ignore the history and stay joined only to the geography. Why not do it? I told myself that I didn't want to permit a feeling of guilt to let me cast aside the history, with its familiar pathos, and happily tumble into this geography, which required no justification other than joy and grace because it offered itself with such generosity.

The temptation was there, and many times I was on the verge of succumbing to the possibility of exchanging the history for the geography. It's even possible that I did so, perhaps for intermittent moments; it's entirely possible I did. They were moments of true peace and sensuality, moments only for myself, unshared and unbroken. Surely during one of these moments it became clear that one could enjoy living with this geography in this way, in this place, but only if history had already played its role, had already outlined its identity, or at least given rise to Jewish identity.

This sensation or experience is one that cannot fail to be repeated. In the geography I find refuge, a friendly refuge, a place where I feel good by myself. It's not a hideout for one in flight but more like a shady place in the rear of a garden, where one finds oneself carried away more by the perfume of newly cut grass than by recollections.

Yes, Israel's geography is ever present, surrounding me, close by, and always within reach of my least effort to seek it out. It is my resting place when the history—the historic presence of this country—overwhelms me. This geography does not contradict the history, but neither does it surrender to it. It maintains the identity of the Jews without forcing them to ask questions about themselves. It's a geography that lightens the ancient heavy burdens of the Jewish heart.

During the time I've been building a life in this country, I have always found in the geography—which is given different names by others—the understanding and support that the Israelis cannot, will not, or don't know how to give. I seize on the geography more than on any other thing or person perhaps because I came here saturated with dialogues and questions, and only the geography preserves me from the return of the nightmares, the nostalgia, and the comparisons.

I believe that one day the relationship I have established with the geography of Israel will lead me toward its men and women. But for the time being the silence in which I live is for me an extension of the geography and it makes me feel peaceful, even happy at times.

But there was one place it was not easy for me to penetrate. I attempted several times yet always remained, for hours and hours, wandering around outside. I studied the place from several angles, under the light at different times of the day or night. I tried to reach a conclusion, but I could never perceive with clarity the magnitudes, the limits, the errors, and the absurdities which that building in Jerusalem that encloses the Holocaust can mean.

There was no great debate with myself. My indecision did not result from any great conflict of ideas or feelings. I simply would have liked to know how I should feel or think about the Holocaust in this country; whether living in Israel establishes a different relationship with the Holocaust; and whether in this country there exists a new reading of the drama, a relationship different from that which developed within me throughout all those years of reading, images, and knowledge.

I rejected each and every recollection and word. I waited patiently for something new to flower in me simply through being in the country which is the only true owner of the dead who are kept in the building amid all possible forms of remembrance and pain.

This notion seemed to mark the beginning of something new. The dead belong to this country. Yet I could not define how, and now it seemed to me that the heritage was more significant than the tragedy—as if the possession could be measured, though the tragedy that was unleashed, and the accumulated pain, was beyond measure.

Lying on a hill with buildings, I stared at that structure and tried to make sense of what was happening to me. I knew, for instance, that I would never find untainted words to calm me. Years and reading had dried up the rivers of words. What was a whirlpool of images, feelings, ideas, and words had become what it was at the beginning—a vast graveyard.

And here I was in Jerusalem, before that graveyard, wanting to start there. Yet I did not want to repeat myself. I did not want to rewrite its history, nor reiterate feelings, nor copy approaches, nor become a professional of the Holocaust. So I searched inside myself for violations of memory to find heroes, not martyrs. I sought to transcend reason and to think of the irrational ones; they only succeeded in altering the pattern of their death, it's true, but at least it was different. I sought the strength to reject the needs and habits that have chained us to this graveyard.

If I entered that building I would surely fall prey to my emotions, into the temptation to weep, into atonement for the images. I would be driven mad by pain and crushed by history. But I felt that, seen from that place, there should be more pain than history.

I asked myself several times whether I was trying to contrast the country with the Holocaust. But no, that wasn't it. I asked myself whether living in Israel did not mean I wanted to erase the two cemeteries I carry inside. In one are buried the mutilations and frustrations that a Jew suffers in the Diaspora, the small and large humiliations that are forgotten so that one can go on, but the inscriptions on the headstones have been erased so as not to remember their meaning: part of the interior burial ground of every Jew in the Diaspora. The other cemetery is of the dead who were the culmination of Jewish history, a silent Jewish nation, more a testimony than a witness to history.

There was nothing in me, however, that led me to flee from that place. I felt clearly that I belonged to that building, to its legitimacy, to its profound design, to its past as well as to its destiny. Yet I didn't know my next step: how to continue my days in this country after having been in that place.

Simple things happened to me, the things that occur in Israel when one spends several days in the same place, or travels several times through the same street. I was spoken to, but people were not surprised that I just stared and did not reply, or merely smiled vaguely. The feeling of identity and belonging is stronger here than the possibilities for communication. That solitude populated by beings that someplace in history were part of my external world allowed me to be passively silent, which was so necessary to me; and at the same time to feel united with children, soldiers, and old people. At one time it even seemed to me that I was in a nation of children, soldiers, and old men, that I could choose for myself any age or any time—as if in Israel there was no rejection of the deep adventures of choice.

I remained fixed to that place of the Holocaust.

Nothing of what is painfully human was missing from the building's contents. I wanted to enumerate that human reservoir, coupling destiny and history, make a detailed catalogue, read it several times, in all directions, silently and loudly, and then ask myself the questions that this country awakens in me. But I was overcome by emotion. I was afraid to quit the place, to withdraw my eyes from that building, afraid that a great interior vacuum would suck me up forever, that forever that seems to await every Jew at the end of an unanswered question. The questions with which Jews flagellate themselves as if the lack of answers—which they pile up by adding question upon question—were the ideal form of survival.

Yet in this country I was surprised to find the pleasure of answers, even the challenge of answers, and many times the happiness of answers.

I understood that if the building neither swallowed nor frightened me, it was because I was ready for the answers. I discovered that this was the first big change in me since my arrival: I was beginning to perceive the answers before the questions. The biggest challenge was in that building.

It was not the least disquieting moment during those days by the building. Dawn came very early and night fell very fast in Jerusalem; the spread of day was indicated by the turning off of thousands of little lights, and that of night by their coming on. But at that moment before the building I was afraid that the interior cemetery, the many graves I brought with me from the Diaspora, held the only accessible answer.

I was there in front of the building in a totally new city with the prestige of antiquity, before a totally new edifice housing the oldest of human tragedies and the most human of pains. I was there, and I should have been leaving aside for a time, without either rejecting or forgetting, all that was past. I should have been striving to find a nexus, a response, that would bring me close to the country, that would make me one with it.

At no time did I think of leaving. This was important in itself. It's a shame I didn't grasp this as it was occurring, because I would have avoided a mass of anguish. But neither was I overwhelmed by feelings, or manipulated by their manicheism.

It was a battle whose duration I cannot measure, but I think I had begun to establish points of equilibrium. The enormities of horror and pain enclosed in the building corresponded with other enormities found within the country.

I could understand that in other countries such pain and horror were the highest signs of Jewish greatness. I saw clearly that very much below, separated by an abyss, the other requirements of daily life had been fulfilled, despite the vast imagination and hope people had exercised to survive in the Diaspora.

I understood that at last I had removed a big tombstone off myself. It wasn't one of those from my interior graveyard, but the huge tombstone which covers the Jews. I could do it because it wasn't a betrayal, or a subterfuge. I had discovered where to place it and not how to forget it. The country could accept the Holocaust as a measure of its destiny, not simply within the framework of remembrance and lament.

Then I went into that building, without ambivalences. I found what all Jews find after seeing the photographs, hearing the narrations and reading the testimonies. I discovered it at the end of the passage inside the building, at a peaceful place we Jews approach with our scarce details, with our murky guidelines. Without asking why, how, or for what there is so much horror. Only asking about somebody, almost humbly, almost without anxiety, and one discovers that there is somebody. That is, there was someone.

There was that someone who was my uncle, Aron Timerman, my father's older brother, murdered October 25, 1942, by Einsatzgruppe C of the German SS, by one or several shots in the back somewhere on the outskirts of a small village in the Ukraine, sometime after his sixty-third year, with the first cold winds striking his upright naked body before he fell dead into the common grave he had helped to dig with his own resigned effort for himself, for his family, for his beloved wife Sheindel, and for other Jews.

The true question—the only valid one, the only one worthy of a reply—was answered. The life of survival here in Israel is the true Jewish destiny. To try to guess at the possibility of survival in remote places, to beg for it with new words, different from those of forty years ago, wrapped in new subtleties and artifices but essentially the same, whether in Princeton or in Paris or in Lima, is almost like complicity with the horror, an irreverence in the face of so much pain.

5

The operation that became a war should have lasted between 48 and 72 hours; so far, 960 hours have passed. It should have resulted in no more than thirty Israeli dead; so far, nearly three hundred soldiers and officers have been buried. (The equivalent for America, relative to population, would be 21,000 killed.) In addition, there are dozens of mutilated, hundreds of wounded. Army communiqués today indicated that, one way or another, the war will continue for many months. The length of active military service is extended and so is the time that reservists will spend on duty. The cost of the war is still difficult to estimate. Nobody knows how the Israeli people will pay for it—with new taxes, inflation, a depreciation of wages and salaries.

When I reply to the detailed questions posed by a friend who has just arrived from Argentina, I try not to influence him. Yet the least I can do is point out that coming to Israel at this time to clarify his Jewish identity could confuse him, because the country itself has begun to debate its own identity. The character of the invasion, the destruction of great cities, has shaken the foundations of the moral structure on which Israel was built. How to apply a moral tradition in the daily life of a nation was an issue Israelis were trying to resolve, some by resorting to religion, others to memory, to need, and to feelings. Any resource was good, but none seemed enough to reduce the confusion. My friend (who must remain nameless because he still lives in Argentina) replied that his identity was a fact in itself, therefore neither the debate nor the confusion impinged on him. He had simply come to see how his own Jewish identity, which had no tradition and no ties, functioned in an Israel of insoluble crises.

I would have preferred that he had stayed in Buenos Aires, but at one time or another the Diaspora descends upon us Israelis. My friend arrived at the worst moment. To blend, in the middle of a war, the feelings and faces he brought with him became, for me, a disproportionate effort. It was possible to rationalize the importance, or perhaps no more than the validity, of the world he brought with him. But how to incorporate it at this moment and feel attracted, as before, to his profound vitality, to his extraordinary and generous humanism?

At the beginning of the sixth week of the war, my friend left to travel through the country. The questions he had formulated about his relationship with Israel had nothing to do with the war. Perhaps it was a mistake to depress him. His points of reference were in the philosophy of a Jewish state, not in the contradictions of Israel. I had also come here motivated by this philosophy, but for me it was impossible to withdraw from the contradictions of daily life—when the daily life of a Jewish nation was precisely the final objective of this philosophy.

Within less than a week, the one ending today, the Prime Minister has declared that the war was pushed beyond his initial objectives by events. The Minister of Defense has declared that for a year he had been preparing the invasion of Lebanon. And the commander in chief of the army has declared that he had been planning the war, including the seizure of Beirut, for eight months.

Possibly the most dangerous aspect of these three versions

of something so shameful as a war is not that two of the three are unavoidably false. What must be worrisome, what should cause concern, is that surely all three must be false: each one of these men was carrying on his own war.

We learn today that the Prime Minister accused the Defense Minister, during a cabinet meeting, of sabotaging a possible American presence in Beirut that would ensure a solution to the problem of the PLO's evacuation. General Sharon needs to crown his victory, and his spokesmen spread the theory that the taking of West Beirut would mean the death of "only" 150 Israeli soldiers.

On these terms begin the irritating and tiring disputes among Israelis. If old scenes could be staged anew, the present debates would be no different from the heated disputes in the backrooms and yards of famous rabbis, one or two centuries ago, over the interpretation of some passage in the holy books.

If it is true that the possibility of a small PLO group remaining in Beirut after the evacuation of the Palestinians indeed threatens the security of Israel, then the lives of 150 soldiers are a small sacrifice. But what if the threat doesn't exist? Even if the threat is there, is war the only answer? Or the best of all?

The majority in Israel feels that war is at once the only and the best solution. The Arabs are partially responsible for this conviction. They proclaimed so many times that the elimination of Israel was feasible that the Israelis came to believe them. Or were the Israelis manipulated into this belief, which in turn made war the only response? The efficiency of the Israeli Army was sufficient in itself, with no need of weighty argument, to "demonstrate" that war was the best solution.

It's very difficult to convince someone who's winning at poker to quit the table. The Israelis give the same impression. It would appear that in a war we only risk the stakes on the table—without considering that meanwhile all other flanks become exposed, among individuals and in the community.

The family of Boaz Evron, a journalist, has been in Israel for five generations. Writing in a Tel Aviv newspaper, he reflects on Israel in these times: "The image of this country, in which all the talent is devoted to the battlefield, is that of a country which thinks all solutions come from the tank and the bulldozer, and this is the worst thing that can befall our society. This country, is it still ours?"

It is ours without a doubt, which is why we are the ones who must change it. It is true, also without a doubt, that all the talent is dedicated to the battlefield; the brightest, the best endowed, and the greatest resources are parceled out among the armed forces and military industry.

Still, in the beginning of the sixth week of the war—and it is already clearly established that after the war we will face an extended occupation of Lebanon—the Israeli Army lost something more important than talent and resources. It lost credibility, the final and deepest reason for its effectiveness: the conviction of each soldier that nothing about the causes and objectives of a war was hidden from him. This conviction freed him to devote his energy and imagination to combat. The efficiency of the Israeli Army was not rooted in the supremacy of its weapons, but in the purity of those weapons.

This loss will have severe repercussions, many of them unpredictable, for Israeli society. It will undoubtedly alter the people's sense of security, in that they will no longer consider the army as the only source of security. It is possible that a larger number of people will begin to consider what it might be like to coexist peacefully with a Palestinian state. It is possible that emigration, now undertaken mostly by youths of military reserve age, will intensify. But it is also possible that the Jewish people will resume their original aims, when their security was guaranteed by a democratic and progressive conception of life. There could be an eruption of the same underlying forces and traditions of the Jewish people that gave birth to political Zionism in the last century.

The new prism through which the army is regarded today

will also affect family life. Many fathers and mothers will ask themselves questions that before this war were hardly ever raised. One such question, which is heard nowadays throughout the land, reveals this mood: Why don't they demobilize my son? What more do they want from him?

It is entirely possible that in the next call to arms fathers and mothers will ask themselves, Why are they taking my son? What will they do with him?

As for the soldiers, in the event of a new war they will race to their bases as always. They will act with the same efficiency. But they will ask their officers more questions than usual, and on the field they will pay more attention to confirming officers' reports and assertions.

We are in the sixth week of the war, and, as during the second week, our minister of defense asks us for a little more patience. Our prime minister continues to be mentally confined to the Europe of the 1930s and '40s. And our mood is more somber than ever, for now we cannot doubt that we have won a war in Lebanon. We already know that no wide range of opportunities is opening before us. It is clear that we are trapped in Lebanon. Israeli experts believe we will spend next winter there—another nine months, during which we will have to provide food, housing, work, education, and health facilities for millions of people, and prevent the different armed groups from murdering each other. We will find ourselves involved in their fights and in their drama. It will be hard to pretend that each house awaiting reconstruction, each child without food, each frustrated and desolate life is not our responsibility; to pretend that the future deaths are not our fault. We have become stuck to Lebanon, to its Muslims and Christians, to its Palestinians and Lebanese.

I believe that an extended period of living together with the Lebanese population will provoke a moral reaction among Israelis. If the border is opened, they will go there to see. If it remains closed ostensibly for security reasons, we in Israel will still know who dies, who suffers, who is hungry and cold. Nowadays our best chance for the future is a move ment of solidarity with the people in Lebanon—Palestinians and others—which surely will become a great Israeli civil movement.

The sixth week begins. Eighty-six reservists, officers and soldiers, have just returned from Lebanon, some on leave, others discharged. No doubt with weariness still in their bones and horror in their souls, they address a letter to the prime minister and to the minister of defense. They demand not to be sent to Lebanon again. They demand the withdrawal of all Israeli soldiers from Lebanon. They demand that the next time they are called to arms, they fulfill their military duty only in Israel, "because we have had enough of killing and of being killed without knowing why." They accuse Begin and Sharon of seeking "to impose a New Order in Lebanon, spilling our blood and the blood of others for the Phalange." They add: "It's not for this that we entered the Army for the Defense of Israel. The war, the lie, and the conquest have no national consensus. Send the soldiers back to their homes."

Yes, the sixth week of war is under way. Outside the Jerusalem building where Menachem Begin has his office, a group of soldiers back from the front maintain a protest watch around the clock. They call for an immediate end to the war and General Sharon's resignation. Their petition is being signed by other soldiers. Anyone who approaches that heavily guarded Jerusalem building can converse with their spokesman. He's a robust redhead, ten years in the paratroops, a veteran of the toughest battles in the 1973 war and in the Lebanon invasion. He's been wounded only once: four days ago, by a group of demonstrators who, incited by the government, tried to dislodge him and his friends. Shuki is studying for his master's degree in history at Hebrew University, and his wife for a doctorate in psychology. This is what he has to say about the Israeli soldier in this war and this postwar: "One gets the mobilization order, and does the best job one can. But then one returns from the war, and one doesn't feel discharged. One has the moral duty to tell the truth about what happened."

The soldiers who come back with the moral need to oppose it, how will they go to the next war? They will go, of course, but how?

A group of academics visit Israel's president to express their concern about the growing breadth and intensity of the debate over the war. They want it postponed until after the war. It's incredible that learned men should voluntarily renounce discussion and dissent. In their own fields they have often confirmed that dissent is the root of all investigation and discovery. It is no less incredible that learned Jews should consider it necessary to clamp one more lock on Israeli society when it is undergoing a crisis. As Jews they must know that grasping the dimensions of the crisis will do more to resolve it than locking it up inside a spiritual ghetto.

A soldier talks to me about a newspaper photograph showing a paratrooper killed in battle. He seems to be resting in his helmet and bullet-proof vest, and about to eat the cherries on a branch clutched in a dead hand. It's not a pleasant picture for the soldier who's talking to me. He lived in a kibbutz and still has a farmer's reactions. He was in Lebanon, too, and he also rested a while in a cherry orchard. The cherries were ripening and had to be picked within a couple of weeks. But a unit that halts in a cherry orchard for an hour's rest before advancing, what can it know or remember of how nature yields its fruits, of the time this takes, of the value of a tree, or even the significance of the face of a farmer? To eat the cherries, soldiers had ripped the branches from the trees and then, as in the picture, sat in the shade with those branches heavy with fruit. The soldier who was talking to me also knew that the lost harvest meant hunger this coming winter, that the torn trees meant many years of hunger. At the time I did not think to tell him that when peace comes he could perhaps return to the orchard and help to restore it. The idea might have made him feel better.

It is a fact that everything that has happened in Lebanon

rebounds on Israel, bit by bit. It emerges in vignettes, like my dialogue with the soldier, in the letters soldiers send their families, in the moral responsibility many soldiers feel for Lebanon's destruction, and in the analyses that many officers make of the army's operations and the value of the captured weaponry. The operations were excessive and not justified by the fighting capacity of the Palestinians, which was inflated by the official propaganda. The weapons were not even enough for a modestly modern army to attack Israel or to defend itself against an Israeli attack.

Accounting for these facts, studying and understanding them within the context of events, will allow Israelis and non-Israelis to arrive at an objective picture of what Israel is today. The still inadequate knowledge of all that has occurred in Lebanon is not the main impediment to the completion of a real picture. The confusion is exaggerated, firstly, because for this country's government each Israeli act of aggression is justified because there was once a Holocaust; and, secondly, because some critics of the government, responding to the same neurotic mechanism, believe that by comparing Israeli actions with those committed by the Nazis, the infamy of the invasion of Lebanon becomes more evident.

Alain Finkielkraut, a young French philosopher, has just pointed out with precision that the debate holds two perils: one, a retreat into a compulsive defense of Israel, into an obsession with denying every condemnation, a compensation of today's doubts with bad faith; second, a reversal of the opinion held about Jews, word for word, to its exact opposite—"Once victims, the Jews have become Nazi executioners."

I believe there is a third peril. If criticism of and accusation against Israel for the invasion are going to be dismissed as expressions of anti-Semitism because they contain verbal images which correspond with Nazi crimes against the Jews, we will become alienated from the world in which we live. Even the anti-Semitic expressions of some critics of Israel's policy do not invalidate the essential facts, nor do they justify our actions in Lebanon. Otherwise we would have to accept Begin's thesis that every act of aggression against Israelis constitutes a continuation of the Holocaust.*

This issue, so widespread in the outside world, is much more limited in the ongoing debate within Israel. I suppose it will diminish even more in the debate that will emerge with the return of those who corroborated for themselves in the field the morality and viability of General Sharon's fantasies.

Those who speak of the Lebanese genocide, of the Nazi-Israeli invader, are expressing their rejection by denying any moral content to the Jewish cause. If the Jews are capable of repeating the barbarities of those who victimized them, then they are not real victims—and the Palestinians deserve the same pity. It is possible that the Jews of the Diaspora are worried by this attitude. They fear losing the barrier, which, they suppose, is made up of shame and guilt among non-Jews. This approach makes the critics lose credibility. To be believed, they must stick to analyzing and measuring the Israeli aggression against Lebanon for what it is, by itself, without borrowing from history emotional and symbolic events and using them out of context.

Just as these critics lose credibility, the application of the same method by some Jewish sectors that follow Menachem Begin's lead makes Jews lose credibility as a people and as history. To compare Arafat to Hitler is an obscene and perverse use of the Jewish tragedy. It must make the younger generations believe that they have been presented with an exaggerated and distorted image of Nazism.

To repeat "Never again," with which we refer to the Holocaust, against the Palestinians, does not mean that the Palestinians have the capacity to exterminate the Jews. But it does

*On August 17, 1982, the Jewish Telegraph Agency reported that two Israeli authorities on the Holocaust, Shmuel Ettinger of the Hebrew University and Yisrael Guttman of the Yad Vashem Institute, protested Begin's excessive use of the term for political purposes.

make one think that the Holocaust must be kept and used in its proper context, so that the contemporary world can establish normal relations with Israel, and vice versa.

The Holocaust and the moral content of the Jewish tragedy have suffered a grave degradation in the hands of those who have used them to justify the invasion of Lebanon in particular, and Israeli foreign policy in general. I sometimes ask myself whether the Holocaust is a right or a mission for those of us who are alive. We must remember the Holocaust to avoid its repetition—against us, or any other people.

Perhaps this war will make us more modest, more humble. Three hundred discharged soldiers meet in Tel Aviv to organize their opposition to the war. They are reservists, their average age thirty-five. It was an effort to leave their families so soon after having been at the front, and participate in the meeting. It wasn't easy, either, to get there in a city without transportation because of the Sabbath. Nor do they have much time to devote to these meetings; all must return to their previous routine. Without the slightest pause they must leap from war to routine. But they think of what they left in Lebanon, and they devote what energy and time they can to demand that the government put an end to the war at once.

They had returned to find their wives tired, exhausted by the effort of caring alone for the home, and by psychological stress. The eyes of their mothers hold proof of silent weeping. Some of their small children had asked whether they were killed in the war. Some missed their exams and now have to seek new examination dates at the university; others must go back to smiling at shoppers in the store, listening to a passenger in the taxi, understanding the instructions of the boss at the factory. Maybe everything is the same, but for them nothing seems the same.

In the tradition of Israeli soldiers, they must visit the families of their comrades killed in combat, and they do so. But they feel betrayed by the government and the army, and on this Saturday night in Tel Aviv they gather together to denounce the conspiracy of silence which has hidden the real objectives of the war, and what has happened in Lebanon during the war.

They set up a board to give continuity to their movement. They are convinced that whether this is to be the last war—and they believe it should be—or whether there will be others every seven or eight years, will depend on what they accomplish in the cities of Israel, and not on the victories that their brains and heroism have achieved in battle.

They appear determined and serene. They will have to integrate all the groups of soldiers and officers who in the past two weeks have come out against the war upon being discharged, particularly the twenty-six air force pilots who sent a joint letter of protest to the Prime Minister. They will have to deal carefully with the appetites of the politicians and their fickleness. Above all, they will have to face the hysterical accusations that they are unpatriotic. In their way, it is what soldiers are already doing when they question General Rafael Eitan, each time he shows up at the front and makes himself accessible, about aspects of the war that they find suspicious—such as, for example, the great human losses in the battle for a segment of the Beirut-Damascus road during the last week of June.

Not one of the government's justifications of the invasion makes the battle and the dead companions necessary. This is also known to the army's chief of staff, who, as the country enters the sixth week of war, reveals a justification unknown until now: Israel fights in Lebanon to win the battle for Eretz Israel—Biblical Israel—not to resolve the problems in Lebanon and Galilee. That Greater Israel which will annex the West Bank and Gaza? What other explanation could he give to skeptical soldiers who have confirmed in the front lines that men were sacrificed for no precise objective? The revelation only serves to increase the soldiers' mistrust.

There is pathos in their task. After the fighting, the heroic deeds and fallen comrades, after the killing of enemies and innocent civilians, these men have proclaimed that all has been in vain. All has been in vain, and yet they can be called to arms at any moment to repeat this new hell we have invented for them: that of deception. They believe a good name for their organization might be "Soldiers against Silence," or "Mobilization against Silence."

It's a special silence. Jorge Luis Borges might have enjoyed toying with it, seeking its remote origins, which surely cannot stem from Judaism. The Jew has explored all the possible meanings of his actions, his dreams, and his words. The intellectual rigor of the Jew cannot admit silence. Nor can he accept the silence of a people who have accomplished all their tasks motivated by just words, never by the irrationality of impulse.

The soldiers understood that by invading a country in an unnecessary war they breached moral limits, and that the extended litany of accusations and lamentations by their chiefs was another facet of the silence. He who hides the just word corrupts it.

I wanted to tell them that they should not feel crushed by the silence. Of all the wrongs inflicted on them, deceit is not the most painful. When they think about it in the weeks to come, they will discover that their posterity was wronged. They went to Lebanon to perpetuate the fire and violence that will envelop their children in the coming wars.

In the years they spent in the military, they were taught to study the feasibility of every action. But in the second week of war they also had to evaluate the tactics they employed. They discovered that the most brilliant actions cost the highest number of dead from their ranks and were unnecessary to achieve what they believed to be the purpose of the war. This will lead them to realize that it was the first war in which the objectives were political.

The importance of engagements, the deployment of forces, the investment of troops and firepower in a determined position were not decided from the military point of view.

After learning this, they need take just a small step to find out the vastness of the scheme in which this war is only the initial event. They will become aware that the deceit imposed on them must lead to a struggle not only for respect for the lives of the soldiers but against the gratuitous use of their lives. It will be a struggle against a military caste; against the degradation of the ethical values of our society and nation; and against the blackmail of the Jewish Diaspora by our government, based on misleading information about Israel's security.

Finally, they will remember from their school days the many projects over the years designed to solve the Jewish problem—from Napoleon's official support of the Jewish community to farm colonies in Argentina, from the autonomous Jewish republic of Birobidzhan in the Soviet Union to total integration a century ago in the Gentile societies of Italy and Germany. All failed because they avoided the answer to the Jewish problem: creation of a national home on the land historically pertaining to the Jews.

This memory, in turn, will allow them to understand that the deterioration of the quality of life in our country, the violence between political parties, the corruption of the economy through the policy of inflation to promote a consumer society, the political use of the army and the lives of its men, and the artificial promotion of confrontation between Ashkenazi and Sephardic Israelis, all will have no solution if we don't take to heart the true character of the Palestinian problem.

This problem will not be resolved by the single fact that we can maintain military superiority, nor because we can invent the most original political formulas. Nothing can replace the need of a people to organize into a state in the territory in which they live and which belongs to them. The alternative our government offers, no matter how it masks it, is to continue repressing the Palestinian people until we destroy their will to live and liquidate their national identity. It's incredible that such a policy is being considered by the very people who demonstrated that this is impossible, that it is immoral, that it is criminal. At any rate, long before we find out whether the policy will work, our society will be destroyed and our people bled by permanent war. Becoming the Prussia of the Middle East is now our manifest destiny—and afterward, what?

We're sick, confused and sad. I feel we should also be very worried. The newspapers today report that General Sharon has wrapped himself in silence within and without the cabinet. He has been lying for several weeks, and the proof is irrefutable. Even when a government tries to hide things, an anguished people unearths information regardless of the level of censorship. We should be concerned because General Sharon has not renounced his plans. He simply delays them, waiting for the moment when he can once again manipulate Israel and the Jewish Diaspora.

Then Sharon will surely tell us that if we invade Jordan and manage to occupy it for three days, despite international opposition, we will be able to establish a "friendly" government in Amman. In keeping with his concept of life, General Sharon finds the collaborationist thesis attractive. We will then have two "allied" Arab governments along our borders: the Lebanon Protectorate and the Jordan Protectorate. We will use these two governments to absorb, into their lands, the Palestinians of the West Bank and Gaza. We will manage those who remain. Our military might will maintain this state of things for ten years, while we take the opportunity to populate the West Bank with Jews.

The protest movements that soldiers are organizing because of the Lebanon invasion will be forced to increase their list of grievances. They have the right to be respected as Israeli citizens, as human beings, as fathers, sons, workers, students, farmers, and teachers. When they begin their demands, they will understand that not one can be achieved if they don't insist on respect for the rights of the Palestinians.

They will discover that they are being led into wars because for many years they have been deceived about the real limits of their security problems, which, though difficult, can be dealt with. They will discover that they were taught to fear the Palestinians because they hate them, though they are told that they hate them because they fear them.

Those who deceive them are the same ones who opposed signing the peace treaty with Egypt. They have always said, and will always say, that peace solves nothing. That is why they maintained that the agreement with Egypt would die with Sadat's death. Wrong. That the agreement would collapse with the first conflict between Israel and an Arab country. Wrong. That Egypt would exchange its smiling face for an aggressive one upon receiving the Sinai. Wrong.

Those who pressured, alienated, and frightened the Israeli people and the Jewish Diaspora at the time, laughing at our principles in the name of their pragmatism, are in the government today; and they want to convince everyone again, even by resorting to a hypocritical use of the Holocaust, that we must be realists, pragmatists. Since we're in Lebanon, let's take advantage of what we have done. The historic problems of the Middle East are resolved with one good army and two strokes of luck.

I receive a letter from New York. Inside is a copy of an article in the *New York Times* by Nathan Glazer and Seymour Martin Lipset. I underline two paragraphs:

> Israel must recognize that it cannot have peace or an end to terrorism without giving the Palestinians the right to self-determination. It must recognize that Palestinian nationalism is as legitimate as Jewish nationalism, and hope that there are ways that this nationalism can find expression without threatening Israel.
>
> The only political outcome of the invasion of Lebanon that would give promise of peace would be an offer by Israel to negotiate with the Palestinians on sovereignty in the occupied areas in which they live. The crucial issue is Israeli willingness to grant real self-determination to the West Bank and Gaza.

6

In political debate it's hard to avoid pejoratives. During the McCarthy era in the United States, the quickest way to define the investigation and prosecution methods of Senator Joseph McCarthy was to call them Fascist. Before World War II, during the student struggles in Buenos Aires—particularly in street demonstrations supporting the Spanish Republic— we shouted "Cossacks!" at the mounted police charging us. After the war, the secret police of Juan Perón's government was dubbed "the Gestapo." More recently, the Naval Mechanics School in Buenos Aires, the main torture and murder center of the military dictatorship, earned the sobriquet of "Auschwitz."

These obvious simplifications are questionable as political science. But they are unavoidable when one wants to convey the quality, instead of the quantity, of political attitudes and political behavior. Fascism and Nazism are the outer limits of man's capacity for physical and ideological violence. It's therefore inevitable that we should resort to them when we want to characterize events for which there are no precise definitions, but which constitute grave expressions of violence. They reveal extreme violations of basic human rights, and awaken feelings of horror and terror.

In a similar way, although we know in detail the extent of state violence in the Soviet Union, we often resort to the expression "Fascism of the left" in order to *feel,* as well as to *understand,* Russia's repressive system.

It goes without saying that the Naval Mechanics School in Buenos Aires cannot be classified as a concentration camp similar to Auschwitz. But how else can the nature of this Buenos Aires military installation be quickly conveyed, where, beginning in 1976, thousands of people were tortured with electric devices, white-hot irons, whips, chains? Where arms and legs were removed with electric saws, wives were raped before their husbands. Bodies, instead of being burned in crematorium ovens, were sent to disappear in the bottom of the sea, dumped from helicopters; children were slain along with their parents, and orphaned infants handed to unknown people. Even this list is not exhaustive, because the humiliation and degradation suffered by prisoners, the violence of the interrogations, the cynical attitude toward relatives who went to the School seeking information must also be included.

I can think of no other recourse than to words that already have a strong meaning. When we are talking about the violation of human rights, the imposition of totalitarian practice on a democratic society, nothing is so clear as the characterization "Fascist." The sole exception, perhaps, concerns ideological persecution; in that case, the first characterization that comes to mind is McCarthyism. This concept is so universal that it has transcended the ideology of the American senator and become a definition of method. There is a McCarthyism of the right as well as a McCarthyism of the left; the latter is not uncommon in France, where the Communist Party regularly tries to quash its intellectual dissidents.

The use of such words is questioned in Israel. It is practically impossible to employ them because of the painful connotations the Holocaust has engraved on the Jewish psyche. Often it is difficult to find a phrase that will quickly define an action or a situation. But with the word "Fascism," the debate centers more on whether it is right to make the allusion than on the merits of the issue. This painful problem began to gain intensity with the formation of Begin's government in 1977, followed by the constant violations of democratic life and of traditional Israeli institutions. It has become more serious in the past two weeks because the government is trying to adapt Israeli society to the needs of the Lebanon invasion, particularly in facing the fact that the country is carrying on its first non-defensive—which is to say, aggressive—war, the longest since the 1948 War of Independence, and the first in which opposition to the war is being demonstrated widely and openly during the fighting.

A few days back, at the beginning of the sixth week, the newspaper *Yediot Ahronot* published the results of an opinion poll which indicated that two out of three Israelis are opposed to the seizure of West Beirut, where the PLO is entrenched, by armed attack.

Today, as we approach the seventh week, a new organization of military reservists opposing the war has held a press conference to announce its program. It calls itself "Yesh Gvul" ("There Is a Limit") and it is launched with a membership of 112 soldiers in the reserve and on active duty. Like all the other soldiers who have organized a protest group, they have sent a collective letter to the Prime Minister and the Minister of Defense demanding an end to the war and the withdrawal of the soldiers from Lebanon. But this is the first group which does not tacitly accept military discipline. When asked whether the movement condones active resistance to service in Lebanon, its members reply that they neither accept nor reject it, that each soldier must decide for himself. Although there have been many instances of soldiers going to prison for refusing to serve in the occupied West Bank territories, this is the first time that a divisive issue has been raised in wartime. A mere four weeks ago it seemed impossible that an attitude similar to that of Americans during the Vietnam War would emerge here. Yet wars accelerate the pace of history faster than we Israelis suppose.

Clearly, everyone needs a simplifying semantic. When the Minister of Defense refers to the dissidence voiced openly, both in the rear guard and at the front, he aggressively states that he will not permit "soldiers' committees" (an obvious reference to those set up in Tsarist Russia's armed forces during World War I to call for withdrawal from the conflict), nor will he put up with the formation of "military juntas" (still another allusion—to the military dictatorships of Latin America's Southern Cone, who, nevertheless, are the best clients of Israel's weapons industry).

Nobody is particularly offended by these metaphors, yet the opposite occurs with any comparison to Fascist methods. But the radicalization of feelings over the war, and the government's use of non-democratic means to gag the opposition, make the resorting to images of Fascism almost inevitable.

Avraham Katz-Oz, a Labor Party deputy and chairman of the Public Audit Committee of the Knesset, has just sent a letter to the Attorney General accusing aides of the Communications Minister, General Mordechai Zipori, of employing Fascist methods. "This is Fascism," he wrote to describe the interrogation of ministry employees to determine their political ideas. Katz-Oz also charged that the ministry's workers are required to spy on each other and report unfavorable talk and comment to General Zipori's aides.

He could have gone on to say that these are anti-democratic, totalitarian schemes. But he could hardly have provided a better description of what this means to Israeli society now and in the future.

In a short article in *Israel Horizons* on the Begin government, the English lawyer Jonathan de Freece, now a resident of Israel and active in politics, tried a scientific approach. He began by quoting an essay by Professor Zeev Sternhell, of the Hebrew University, who asserts that "Fascist ideology took on the character of an anti-intellectual reaction which pitted feelings and emotion, and irrational forces of every kind, against the rationality of democracy. It was the rediscovery of instinct, the cult of physical strength, violence and brutality . . . its aims were to create a world of fixed criteria, a world freed from doubt and purged of all foreign accretions. . . ."

This definition applies to the methods employed by Begin, and it also describes some of the developments that have emerged within Israeli society since the occupation of Arab territories in the 1967 Six-Day War. Still, I believe that many of the accepted tools of political analysis cannot be applied in Israel today, even with every scientific precaution, without igniting a debate over form and, as a result, disguising the real depth of the problems afflicting Israeli society.

Because Israel has a permanent high profile in international debates, and because Israel is judged by highly diverse standards, it is impossible to find a consensus. Beyond that, another factor adds to the confusion, to the controversy: the occupation of disputed territory by its own people. Consider Britain between the two world wars. There was democracy at home for its own citizens; but its colonies could only perceive Britain as an imperial power whose prerogatives had nothing to do with democracy.

For me, as an Israeli citizen, Israel is a democracy. Yet it is precisely as an Israeli that I have a duty to remain alert about the stability of its democracy and the risks it faces. In this sense, it is evident to me that Israeli democracy is threatened by the Begin government, whose policy is not democratic and whose actions are establishing the basis for another kind of country: a totalitarian country which, like all totalitarianisms, cannot be likened to any other. There is nothing more national than a specific totalitarianism. Its ideas, its methods, and its psychology are always profoundly national. This typical quality is its guarantee of subsistence.

On this point, I would say that the Begin government is reactionary and anti-democratic—if any kind of definition or qualification is necessary.

To be sure, it's not hard to draw up a long list of things in Israeli life that can only exist in a democracy: an independent judiciary, a free press, no special security police devoted to violent repression and state terrorism, freedom of academic inquiry, free political parties, a free parliament, fair elections, ideological pluralism, freedom of assembly, an independent labor movement, and much more.

But the question that must be asked is: Which of these attributes of Israeli society are respected by Begin's policies and which ones are eroded? I am thinking of the long period during which Juan Perón governed Argentina. Each of the three times he attained the presidency, he won in free elections by a substantial or even overwhelming majority—between fifty-five and seventy per cent of the vote. There was a parliament, political parties, and so forth; he never committed fraud in the elections. Yet the dynamic of his government smothered democratic life and undermined democratic institutions, until it became evident that he was using the democratic system for anti-democratic ends.

This is the crucial problem when politicians without a democratic ideology achieve a majority, whether by direct elections, as in Perón's case, or by agreement among parties for a coalition government, as in Begin's case.

In the last few years, Israel has lost many of its democratic qualities, particularly since the Lebanon invasion.

New concessions to intolerant religious groups not only impede the modernization of social life but reduce the scope of secular activities, especially in the crucial field of education. Economic policy is characterized by the irresponsibility of demagogic governments. Financial speculation takes the place of productive investment; uncontrolled issuance of currency devalues its worth, ignites inflation, and promotes the consumption of unnecessary goods to maintain the government's popularity. Budget increases go to swell the bureaucracy, and hiring is done on a strictly partisan basis. Investment for research, which could help to increase technological exports, is reduced; reduced, too, is investment for housing, highways, and health care. Funds are used instead for the illegal establishment of businesses in the occupied territories.

The state has abandoned numerous projects in which the secular population participates, failing to fulfill its obligations to farming cooperatives, to specialized industries, and to new settlements within pre-1967 Israel. Such neglect has caused a wave of emigration that is reaching dangerous proportions.

The dynamics of such policies will undoubtedly alter the nature of Israel. The society will become more closed, more intolerant, more fundamentalist. When these conditions, which are contrary to the spirit and letter of the country's fundamental charter, are being introduced by a partisan coalition in government, we are face to face with an anti-democracy. For such substantial changes in society a democracy requires a broad debate leading up to a vote. But the way things are accomplished in Israel constitutes an anti-democratic exercise by a merely circumstantial majority. Thus it is a dictatorial act, even though by a dictatorship of the majority; it is the expression of a totalitarian ideology.

There is no better reflection of the substantial change in the character of the country by apparently democratic means than Israel's annexation of East Jerusalem and the Golan Heights, on the Syrian border, which were seized in the Six-Day War.

The annexation of these territories means conditioning Israel to a state of permanent conflict in the Middle East, reinforcing its character as a militarized nation. Such a decision should not even be reached by a parliamentary majority. In a democracy certain decisions are beyond the scope of political institutions. They should be the result of a broad and specific debate, of a process involving all citizens. Neither can a policy of surreptitious but obvious annexation of the West Bank be carried out by administrative measures, without a national debate and a national consensus. The case of the West Bank is more than grave. It demands a social and economic effort that is not only bleeding the country but chaining future Israeli generations to its defense.

The Begin government considers that the unlimited power of a parliamentary majority is one of the characteris-

tics of a democracy. Begin himself cannot seem to understand that respect for the rights of minorities is no less important, that not even the broadest interpretation of democracy
allows for the transformation of a society solely by the power
of a parliamentary majority.

There is no need to analyze Israel's policy in the occupied
territories in detail; the daily reports in the mass media provide sufficient illustration. Establishing a democratic formula
for occupation is indeed difficult. After World War II, the
Allies were able to accomplish it in Germany, Austria, and
Japan, but they had no territorial appetites for those countries. When Israel made it manifest that its objective was the
addition of the occupied territories, which means reducing
the Muslim population to second-class status, it undertook an
action unacceptable to a democracy.

Shortly before his death in 1980, the historian and philosopher Jacob Talmon wrote an open letter to the Prime Minister entitled "The Country Is in Danger" in *Haaretz,* a Tel
Aviv newspaper. He did not use the concept of "country" in
the absolute sense of extreme nationalists. Talmon was referring to the basic values of his country, and he made clear that
what he saw in mortal danger was Israeli democracy.

Regarding our policy toward the occupied territories,
adopted by a parliamentary majority which the government
considers a sufficient democratic mandate (and which I consider insufficient, because a national mandate would be the
only democratic avenue), I quote from Talmon's letter:

> However lacerating are the pain and the shame we feel
> for the affronts that our perverse and anachronistic pol-
> icy, which is devoid of a future, causes among our neigh-
> bors, much greater and even incisive is the fear of the
> consequences of such behavior for us, the Jews; for our
> dream of a social and moral rebirth, one of the most
> aesthetic and ethical aspects that characterized Zionism
> among the national liberation movements. The aspira-
> tion to be the master, which is always accompanied by

fear of the unity and rebellion of the servants, causes compulsions which are stronger than all the good intentions. Amid the reality of a permanent state of emergency, of continual alert and fear, of terror and counter-terror, and of the escalation of hostilities, nobody can escape the rigors of amoral stratagems, of dissuasive strikes, of reprisals, and all this then becomes a system of government, a style of life and relationships which throttles and perverts both parties at the same time. Thus the instincts of aggression and evil that even a normal government can barely control are given a free rein. Creativity, the happiness of life, the tenderness of feelings are oppressed in such an atmosphere.

Professor Talmon was describing precisely the changes that Israel is experiencing because of its policy toward its neighbors. These changes neither expand nor maintain the country's democracy, but instead cause it to deteriorate and diminish.

In a way, Professor Talmon was with us during this war. Naturally, he was not heeded by the Prime Minister; but in the third week of the invasion, the Israel Academy of Sciences and Humanities, Hebrew University, the Israel Historical Society, and the Van Leer Foundation held a symposium in Talmon's memory entitled "Totalitarian Democracy and After."

The government undertook the invasion of Lebanon with the greatest number of violations of democratic methods to date, all of them concentrated in a brief span of time. The most striking, of course, was to lead the country into a war with a massive deployment of men and weapons while concealing that it was actually fighting a war. But beyond the trickery there was premeditated deceit when the Prime Minister told the Knesset that the advance into Lebanon had limited objectives.

From that moment on, the thwarting of the Knesset entailed—insofar as it is a forum for debating a development as momentous as a war—a virtual liquidation of the Knesset. The Prime Minister and the Minister of Defense continually avoid meetings of the Foreign Affairs and Defense Committee, and when they deign to reply to the deputies' questions, they provide false information. We are about to enter the seventh week of the war, and Parliament remains impotent. The government does not believe in the rights of the minority, which means that it doesn't believe in the existence of a sizable number of citizens. It holds to the idea of a centralized Israel, of a totalitarian Israel. All this inspires the former foreign minister Abba Eban, now a deputy, to protest in a letter that "the situation has no precedent in the history of the Foreign Affairs and Defense Committee, and it is unacceptable."

Just now, after more than a month of fighting, the Knesset has discovered an ordinance enacted by the Minister of Defense at the start of the war, which, among other things, authorizes senior army officers to arrest any person anywhere outside Israel. In making the charge, Deputy Shulamit Aloni pointed out that the legal anomalies in the wording of the ordinance indicate that General Sharon has virtually created a military government in Lebanon outside the laws of Israel and Lebanon, and outside international law.

Despite all its efforts, the opposition cannot get the government to accept the rights of the Parliament, an indication that the institution has reached a point where it is no longer a guarantee of democracy in Israel.

Deputy Yossi Sarid has demanded to know why the government and army officers exaggerated the quantity and quality of the weapons seized from the PLO in Lebanon. Sarid's repeated questions remain unanswered. He charged that there was an attempt to create a false impression of imminent threat to Israel's northern border. For instance, instead of five hundred modern tanks, there were only ninety obsolete T-34s, which could fire their weapons but were not mobile. These same army officers, Sarid pointed out, told delegations of Diaspora Jews who raise funds for

Israel that the captured weapons could have equipped one million terrorists, which amounts to a paranoid fantasy. Sarid is requesting an investigation, but there is little likelihood it will ever be held.

This raises one of the most complex problems of Israeli life: our relationship with the Diaspora. If, instead of Deputy Sarid, those questioning the Israeli government were the deceived foreign Jewish leaders, their public inquiries would strengthen and support democracy in Israel. But the evident paralysis of the Diaspora when it is manipulated by the Israeli government, and the use by the Begin government of this paralysis, is additional evidence of the government's totalitarian character.

Two years ago Professor Talmon, in his open letter, foresaw this situation, and warned: "Mr. Chief of Government: The policies of your government are turning Israel into a clandestine sect that incites the Jews of the Diaspora to recant the liberal principles which allowed them to achieve their influential standing and which are, for them, a lifelong doctrine to which they have adhered with abiding faith."

As so often happens in Israel, the characterization of its policies raises, at least in public opinion, two apparently contradictory problems. One of Israel's greatest international triumphs, particularly in its relationships with the United States, has been to maintain its standing as the only democracy in the Middle East. For more than thirty years Israel has upheld its democracy, stable and immutable, as one of its principal claims to the support of the Western world. And from an international point of view, it's true, Israel is the only democracy and internally stable country in that turbulent region.

But since Begin took over, Israel's commitment to democracy has suffered a serious deterioration. For one thing, the nation's policy toward Golan, the West Bank, and Gaza has destabilized the Middle East. Not even the peace treaty with Egypt helped to alter this situation, because it was only one part of the Camp David accords, and the total application of the accords is the only way to establish a peaceful and democratic resolution of the region's conflicts. By avoiding time after time the fulfillment of the accords' provisions for the autonomy of the West Bank and Gaza, the Begin government has not behaved like a democracy. The invasion of Lebanon, a direct consequence of the Begin government's policies, has seriously tarnished Israel's image in the West.

The second problem is that internal conflict has also diminished Israeli democracy. While Israeli foreign policy requires that the country be upheld as the sole practicing democracy in the Middle East, this need cannot be turned into an instrument of pressure, and even blackmail, against Israeli citizens. The offensive of the Begin government against Israeli democracy is constant; it responds to an ideology, and to tactical considerations; and it is changing Israeli society. The average Israeli citizen cannot do less than denounce this conflict that affects his daily life and his future. The charge that his open protests and political activities somehow weaken the notion that Israel is the sole democracy in the Middle East cannot become a pretext for calling citizens to silence. On the contrary, these citizens, even if they are a minority, are the ones striving to preserve Israel's democratic character against a government that is undermining it.

Just today there was revealed one of the ways in which the government increases its parliamentary majority, giving it a greater capacity for maneuver by obvious democratic means, but in exchange for obviously anti-democratic measures.

In order to add to the ruling coalition the three deputies of the right-wing nationalist Tehiya Party (opposed to the Camp David accords and to the treaty with Egypt), thereby creating a majority of 64 votes in the 120-member Knesset, the government will agree to an increase in the number of Jewish businesses in the West Bank and Gaza, to new industries there; and, in the event that local Arab councils ever win a measure of autonomy, they will never be granted any voice in the administration of land and water resources. This small faction, in turn, has agreed to postpone for the time being its demand that the occupied territories be annexed, but it insists that the local communities remain under Israeli sovereignty.

To any charge that such impositions on the occupied territories cannot come from a democratic nation, the government, as always, will reply by evading the real issue, and, instead, will present the evidence of its enlarged parliamentary majority.

Faced with the demands of the government as it seeks to continue its slow annexation of the occupied territories, the Israeli citizen has no choice but to accuse the authorities of destroying democracy, of turning Israel into an aggressive and potentially totalitarian nation.

At the same time, the social, cultural, and economic concessions that the government grants to intolerant and totalitarian political parties with the sole purpose of remaining *democratically* in power also force the Israeli citizen to denounce the loss of democracy that is affecting his life.

To be sure, the confusions and conflicts that exist in Israel tempt one to reach for semantic simplifications. But I think one does more justice to reality if one calls Israel a parliamentary republic and not a democracy.

Despite the foreign policy use of the "only democracy" theme, the Begin government needs to deny at home that international opinion has any influence whatsoever on its decisions. This way it keeps a chauvinistic climate alive, which is the basis of its domestic policy. Thanks to this manipulation, the prime minister has managed to extirpate the goodwill many sectors of the Western world have had for Israel. The invasion has set on a firm foundation the changes in Israel's image, the object of polemics in the West even before the onslaught.

In his open letter, Professor Talmon told Menachem Begin:

I recall a meeting organized by the Foreign Minister at the time (I refer to 1969) between Hebrew University professors and the Defense Ministry. When I was invited to give my views, I was compelled to say that as a historian—whose diagnosis, like that of a physician, should not be influenced by personal opinion and must be based solely on objective elements—I could do no less than point out that I did not know of a single case of such a complex conflict, so permeated by emotional and irrational elements, by fears, terrors and desires of vengeance, as ours is, which had been resolved without the outside intervention of a single power or several powers interposing their counsel, their influence, their mediation, pressure and impositions. And in a recent conversation with a brilliant Israeli diplomat, we both agreed that history will not forgive the United States for not having taken a hand in the conflict long before 1973, as would have been proper for the leading power at the time. . . . During the last few years Israel has been profiled as rebellious against the international system. In our country it is easy to reap applause by railing against evil Gentiles, against the obtuseness and selfishness of nations. But these generalized recriminations, which are not without foundation, do not explain things, nor do they enable us to advance one millimeter.

Since Professor Talmon presented his analysis in 1969, Israel has gone through three wars—Yom Kippur, the War of Attrition, and Lebanon. Since he wrote "The Country Is in Danger" in 1980, Begin's policy has taken Israel to the present war. Perhaps the moment has come for the Jewish communities in the Diaspora, and especially in the United States, to study Jacob Talmon's patriotic efforts with great care and to take note of the importance of his participation in the preservation of Israeli democracy—and of Israel's security.

7

My friend returned to Tel Aviv. I asked him nothing about what he had done. He told me nothing. I said he seemed like Meursault forty years later. Albert Camus's character had been a stranger in his own Algiers; more than that, a stranger in his city, in his street, in his room. The Friend, as I came to think of him, equally alone, would not have been this type of stranger, not even in the Foreign Legion.

He laughed when I described my thoughts to him. He asked for more details, but I didn't have many more. I was improvising. I reminded him that Meursault believed that everything was indifferent to him only because a great terror separated him from life. He feared that he would be indifferent to life. Any Freudian could have told him that he confused life with his mother. This was in 1942. I suppose that in 1982 the Stranger would have discovered his identity starting from a real interest in life, without fear and without waiting for life itself to accept and approve of a Stranger. If Meursault believed he was liberated from all demands because he was a fatalist, my friend considered all demands part of destiny, and he felt invaded by a great happiness in the effort of making his destiny explicit. If for a Frenchman in Algeria in 1942 resignation assumed the shape of indifference, and indifference in turn diluted the anxiety that makes one face reality, then, it occurred to me, for a Jew in Buenos Aires in 1982, resignation consisted in accepting the identity and the conflicts inherent in the act of acceptance. His own resignation had led Meursault, in the final effort, when he accepted the death he awaited, to say: ". . . for the first time I opened up to the indifference of the world." But when a Jew in Buenos Aires, in 1982, wants to carry his resignation to its final stage, he has to realize that if the guillotine was for Meursault the "indifference of the world," arrival in Israel was its culmination for the Friend.

"Then in 1982 Camus's Stranger would be a Jew?" he asked.

"Inevitably."

"But according to Jewish tradition, I'm not one," the Friend retorted with a smile. "My mother was a Christian."

I believe that he didn't want to go into the subject. As always, he was more alert to the possibility of gathering facts, points of view, topics.

I was not disheartened, and went on: "This makes you the perfect Stranger forty years later. A Stranger because you are a Jew, a Stranger because you're not a Jew. A Stranger because you believe that you have *your place* in life, and finding it will be enough. But once you find it, it will make you a Stranger to the rest of humankind. In brief, you are the Stranger who has never been and will never feel the Stranger because, for you, life is identity and destiny. The world's indifference is, for you, sufficient reason to seek destiny, just as it was for Meursault to seek the guillotine. Forty years later you have a good identity. What does it matter if you are Christian? In these times only a Jew can move with such ease in the realm of destiny and identity. But to accomplish this, one must choose—and you have made a choice. After a life of pleasant experiences, you arrived here, not some other place. It was a perfect choice. Perhaps as perfect as Meursault's in his indifferent assassin's cell."

While talking, I toyed with a straw fan made by Arabs in

a village near Jerusalem. It was an evening in the middle of July, and the heat was even more unbearable because of the *jamsin,* the desert wind, which had been blowing all day. We were sitting on the balcony of my house in Tel Aviv; my wife had placed a pitcher of iced orange juice on the table.

The Friend looked away several times as I talked. I don't think it was because he was bored. Possibly he was anxious, perhaps he thought of his wife. I too resort to this mental device when anguish wells up in me during a conversation: I think of my wife, who will always be there, who neither doubts nor arouses doubts. I don't believe I made him uncomfortable, or even caused him to examine himself from a new perspective. No, if there was anything at all, it was a touch of anxiety, that sort of anxiety which is sweet and tender because it doesn't produce fear. I always envied the Friend's ability to enjoy the anxiety produced by certain ideas and situations. Certainly there was no panic, no fear, not even a slight tremor.

He uncrossed his legs and arose from the canvas chair into which he had sunk comfortably. He leaned on the railing of the balcony and looked out at the Mediterranean spread before us, just beyond a dusty little hill.

Almost since the beginning of the invasion, the evening sun has been redder than ever, and the entire sky is invaded by a violent red that doesn't vanish when the sun finally sinks beneath the sea. This has been happening for several weeks, and everyone wants to see a sign, a message. It could be a mass of dust floating in the sky, according to the experts. But it is tempting to believe that it is the smoke of gunpowder over Beirut, which is moving to the south and west.

The Friend remained silent for a while, eyes fixed on that red sun. He wore a short-sleeved white shirt, lightweight dark blue pants, and sandals. His strong arms were bronzed. He fit perfectly into the Israeli landscape. Still with his back to me, he extended his arm toward the north and said: "I'll live in Tantura, by the sea."

An Israeli would have told him that he had made the right

decision—to live in Israel. It is always the right decision to settle in Israel. But I still felt a certain diffidence. It seemed as though by approving his decision, I would be engaging in a form of self-approval. Generally when somebody tells me of such a decision, I remark that I hope he's sure of what he is doing because it is an important decision, that he should consider that Israel may not live up to his expectations; but that once he is certain, he will lead a life of transcendental contentment. Finally, it's never easy, and sometimes the conversation turns into a bitter argument which we end by agreeing upon the intrinsic values of the existence of Israel and of living here.

But I said nothing, almost nothing, to him.

"Tantura is a small place on the coast, closer to Haifa than to Tel Aviv," he said.

"I've never been there," I replied. "I should live on the coast. I don't know why I don't."

"My wife will love it. We'll have a garden."

"Come on," I said. "Let's be honest. What are you telling me? You simply come here in the middle of this war, a young man of thirty in search of your identity, and, just like that, find a place to live in. No doubts, no memories, no tragedies, not even a small anti-Semitic incident in your youth, and, naturally, not even a tiny reference to a distant relative who disappeared in the Holocaust. Just like that, so easy, a Latin without agony or terrors. You went to look for something in Europe, but when the war broke out, why not come to see a bit of war in Israel and feel fortified because Jews handle weapons so well?"

I stopped for a moment. I didn't understand why I was attacking him. Perhaps for some people—among them the Friend—Israel is not an eternal open wound on his breast.

"Just like that," I went on. "Catholic, Apostolic, and Roman mother, Jewish father. So easy."

He said nothing for a little while. Then: "No, it's not easy. But neither is it traumatic."

We talked for another thirty minutes, and I became clearly

aware that he could be happy in Israel. His pragmatism would be a good frame for his illusions. Some confuse pragmatism with cynicism. That's a mistake. At any rate, there was nothing of the cynic in the Friend. Even when he finally opened up to Israel's tender indifference, just as Meursault had opened up to the world's tender indifference, like Camus's character he would content himself with no response because he expected nothing special from Israel, just as Meursault expected nothing from life. The two strangers were looking for identity, and they found it. That was all they needed.

When we said farewell, I thought I would never see him again. In me, illusions were stronger than Israel. I supposed our conversation would trouble him. At any rate, his parting words to me were:

"I'm more Israeli than you are."

But I believe he is mistaken. It's possible I have changed, but it is because we are in the seventh week of war and have discovered that not only did we never know the nature of the war in which we are involved, but something graver still is happening to us: we don't know what kind of diplomacy represents us, what kind of cease-fire protects our soldiers, what sort of future awaits us. We don't even know whether the continuity of the country we considered our own will be maintained. These are fears that the Friend and his wife will feel only after their first child is born in Tantura, and if they are still here for the next war.

The Friend does not talk to soldiers who have been discharged in the last few days. While we were awaiting their return home, it never crossed our minds that many of them had already been given orders to rejoin the army on specific dates—within forty, sixty, or seventy days. We don't know why or what for. They don't, either. This is why we don't know what kind of war we're involved in. We can't even say that the war will end when we defeat the enemy, because although we know where the enemy begins, we don't know where he ends. We can't say that the war will end when there are no more enemies within our borders, because although we know only too well where our borders begin, we don't know where they end.

As to the continuity of the country, we Israelis must rekindle the struggle so that this continuity will retain the ideals that gave birth to this nation. The letters in the newspapers, the denunciations by soldiers, the length of the war, the hardships of daily life, the lack of confidence in government announcements, skepticism over the army's reports, are all new elements that add confusion, and, above all, sadness— the sadness of having been cheated—to the worries for relatives at the front.

Soldiers say that some high officers, including generals, have asked them that, in the event they sign letters of protest against the war, they do so as civilians and not as members of the armed forces. Soldiers also recount jokes passed around at the front and at military bases:

One Palestinian tells another, Israelis must think we're birds because every time they fire into the air, a Palestinian falls to the ground.

Of the three drivers in General Sharon's service, the one who drives him to Beirut says that the troops must be ordered back to Israel; the one who drives him to bases far from Beirut says that it's too early to make a decision and best to wait; but the one who drives him in Israel says we should seize Beirut and the losses be damned.

Israel's continuity was based on the impossibility of an officer ever trying to influence the opinions of a soldier, on the absence of bitter jokes about Palestinian reality, on the possibility of a consensus on a war. Our country was the framework for our Jewish continuity, for our spiritual continuity. Now we have lost it. The French journalist Jean Daniel, whose support of Israel has been as steadfast as his criticism of our oppression of the Palestinians, pointed out something quite simple: "Israel is a country like any other." It's hard to resign ourselves to this notion, although many people in Israel, perhaps a majority, are at ease with the idea.

I ask myself whether they would be equally at ease if they were not always the military victors, or if we were to be routed diplomatically. Would we then cease to be a country like the rest, and fall back on the memories of the Holocaust so as to appeal to the guilt feelings of other nations? It's curious—though perhaps not so very curious—that the most belligerent Israelis and Diaspora Jews are those who resort to the Holocaust with greatest frequency, who have the greatest tendency to claim the pity of the other nations, who are most disposed, in case of need, to pronounce that Israel is not a country like any other.

No, Israel is not like other countries; or, if you prefer, it shouldn't be. It was created not to be. The best guarantee for its security lies in maintaining the ideas of its founders. As the philosopher Jean-Pierre Faye wrote in *Le Monde:* "This is the Begin government, the Begin state. The Zionist state cannot be attacked because of Begin's policy."

The debate developing in Israel creates a sadness that permeates everything. When it affects our sense of continuity, it alters our notions of security, upsetting our lives, our relations with those near and dear, and our questions and answers.

Continuity is more than a few official proclamations on identity, more than the fireworks the Diaspora displays to highlight the memory of our tragic history. Continuity is what Yaakov Guterman expressed for us all in a letter to the Jerusalem *Post* that many of us keep out on the table. Just now when my son has been discharged from the army, I read it carefully and slowly, and I think about what it says and ask my wife to think about it with me. I still don't dare to discuss it with other people. I think my Argentine Friend would not understand it. Not yet. He would assume I was reading it to convince him not to settle in Israel. The truth is exactly the opposite: I'm more than happy that he decided to come. I believe that Guterman's letter is an invitation to Israel, to assume our true continuity:

"I am the descendant of a rabbinical family, the only son of Simha Guterman, a Zionist and Socialist who died as a hero and a fighter against the Nazis in the Warsaw uprising. I was rescued from the Holocaust and brought to Israel; I served in the army and built my home in Israel.

"A son was born to me, called Raz—a son who grew up to be a great pride to his family, strong and beautiful and honest and upright in his character. Despite personal misfortunes and difficulties, I raised him with unending love and affection and with great pride as a father. In my secret thoughts, I saw him as a link in the chain of history, and in his being and character, along with others like him, the realization of our people's renewal.

"When the time came for him to join the army, he volunteered, in the spirit in which he was educated, for one of the special units, one of the most challenging units of the army, and there he served with great effort and devotion. He was due to be released in a few weeks and his plans were many.

"Along with my son and his friends, I was aware of the government's intentions, and we lived in constant fear. Every night, I went to bed with a prayer in my heart that war might be avoided.

"Every child knows that Menachem Begin and Ariel Sharon sought a reason to break into Lebanon to instigate the first war that was not a war of defense. They sought to undo, with this questionable military victory, all their failures, inadequacies and frustrations.

"I remained with a prayer in my heart that reasonable and concerned people in Israel and abroad would prevent them from this madness, but my desire and the desire of the sons was not fulfilled.

"The bullet fired in London caused them to send lethal war machines to spread death into the cities of Lebanon and its villages. When the Katyushas returned fire, the hour they had been waiting for impatiently finally arrived.

"With unabashed effrontery, Menachem Begin, Ariel Sharon, Rafael Eitan, and the ministers who voted for the war in Lebanon sloganized *Peace for Galilee* when there had been no shots fired in Galilee for over a year.

"My son Raz, my beloved son, and his friends were sent

with their unit, in great haste and frenzied irresponsibility, to bloody battle to take the Beaufort. He was the first one to break through the trenches leading to the fortress. He fought valiantly and there he found his death.

"Thus was severed the chain of unending Jewish generations, ancient and full of heroism and suffering, and thus was cut off the flowering of a life that was just beginning to blossom.

"And thus they caused the destruction of my whole world.

"How many years would it have taken the Palestinian terrorists to kill and injure so many Israeli soldiers as these people did in the course of one week of this damnable war? How much loss and mourning have they caused?

"Even before the blood was dry on the rocks of the mountain of Beaufort, Begin and Sharon hurried into their helicopters, surrounded by photographers, motion-picture cameras, and microphones, to declare and sound forth with vanity. They did not even ask forgiveness for the mistakes or the dark devices of their nationalistic schemes and their adventurous irresponsibility.

"And the voice of our sons' blood cries from the ground!

"And if they have only a spark of conscience and humanity, may my great pain pursue them forever, the suffering of a father in Israel whose world has been destroyed and the joy of life destroyed in him forever."

It seems ridiculous that in the seventh week of war we're still immersed in the nostalgia of the first three days. Against all logic we Israelis believed—many because they wanted to believe—that the war could be over in three days. All too soon we found that we had been lied to, and that we had lied to ourselves. This conviction has now become a collective mood, which transcends analysis and knowledge. This long war, much too long, affects every aspect of our lives as a people. It becomes a spiritual encumbrance even when we don't want to think about it. It is growing in our flesh. Without being able to explain why with any clarity, I fear that it can transform the entire way of being and thinking of a people.

While the Israeli avoids saying so to himself, he perceives that there is no military solution to his security problems. It is futile to remind him that all the European fantasies of collective security based on the strength of bayonets led to World War II. In Israel's case, the application of such historical references means becoming mired in sterile controversy. The Israeli only accepts analysis of his situation if it is conceded that his is unique. Even then, he must be reminded that bayonets can be used for many purposes, but one can't sit on them. He knows that coming up are long months during which he will have to remain perched on bayonets, and the months he will spend in the ranks of the army have been extended beyond his capacity to keep on fighting. Even then, what is actually creating this state of general disgust with ourselves, of nostalgia for something we seem to have lost only a brief while ago, is the realization that the most perfect expression of our national will, our military might, will not resolve the Palestinian problem, which is our biggest national issue.

The Palestinian camps in Lebanon, veritable suburbs on the outskirts of Tyre and Sidon, are no longer barred to journalists in the seventh week of the war.

Although every moment of the day we recite the long list of mistakes made by the Palestinians and then go on to the long list of crimes committed by the PLO, not even the Israeli's obsession with his own security can ever justify the indiscriminate destruction of Palestinian camps. Evidence of the army's ferocity is now penetrating through the armor of Israeli fear. Moreover, there is the depressing knowledge that the war will be with us for a long time, and in different shapes; and the conviction that, even though he still tries to fool himself, there is no military solution to the Palestinian problem; and the need to assimilate into his psyche the knowledge of the destruction and tragedy we have wrought in Lebanon; and besides all this, the soldiers returning from the front this seventh week—a week of replacement of troops—speak to us of the existence of the other, the Palestinian. And whether we like it or not, we must accept what the soldiers tell us. The right of an Israeli soldier to bear witness is hard to deny. In their testimony these men display unexpected feelings. Their amazement is understandable, but at times it even suggests a kind of envy, a curious envy.

The soldiers came to know that region which is so difficult to penetrate: the affective world of the others. They brought back with them stories about families of up to ten relatives helping each other to survive amid collapse and panic. Stories about children completely different from the rocket-launching children who were the only ones mentioned by official Israeli propaganda. Lost children of ten or twelve caring for their younger brothers, and for old people, begging food for their families; children who didn't cry, who don't engage in mischief because they already have the somber seriousness of age. They met Palestinian youths who served as volunteers in hospitals, who have friends, who want to have children some day, and, who, like the Israelis, dream of a motorcycle, of a girl; youths who are also proud of being unafraid of death and who also mourn the death of others. They brought back stories of nurses who remained with the wounded, of doctors who did not flee; and they encountered Palestinian youths who, like themselves, did not ask for mercy and did not humble themselves.

These soldiers saw that Palestinian youths, like themselves, feel pride in their identity. It is an identity that official propaganda had told them was shapeless, undefined, confused, nearly paranoid, almost criminal. The soldiers found it no more confusing than their own; they did not hear the Palestinians utter more painful or complex questions than those that cause them such anguish in Israel. When they heard Palestinians speak of that country which they will have some day, they heard faint echoes of the reminiscences of their own parents and grandparents about earlier times in Israel.

Or, hearing such dreams, perhaps they felt a tinge of envy.

When the soldiers came back to Israel in the seventh week of the war, they discovered that everyone knew of their heroic acts. But with them they brought, besides their own anguish, euphoria, or weariness, the exploits, the heroism of the sacrifices of the other, of the Palestinian with whom, at one time or another, they had the chance to speak for the first time.

The Dutch historian Johan Huizinga wrote that "every epoch sighs for a better world. The more profound the despair caused by the chaotic present, the more intimate is the sigh."

When the Israeli says that the war will never end, it's his intimate sigh for the end of this war, for making it the last war. Even deeper than the desire for a better world is the nostalgia for that world. It is as if he wants to recover something he already had. There is an intuition—almost a conviction, almost a presentiment—that the Palestinians have changed their place in our lives. That the difficult effort of understanding that place and all its implications await us. We are amazed to find that the idea does not dismay us.

A play that can be seen these days at the Festival of Jewish Theater at Tel Aviv University is entitled, significantly, *Imagining the Other*. There are three Arab actors and three Jewish actors. Toward the end the three Arabs intone an Israeli patriotic song that takes the form of a ballad. It expresses the Jewish desire to return to Zion, and its reference to the land of milk and honey turns the ballad into a religious canticle. The Israeli critic Zvi Jagendorf writes in his review of the play: "Are they making fun of a Zionist hymn? No. Are they making its harmonic yearning include them? Perhaps. Are they making us aware of their presence as the *others* in our lives, our shadows? Certainly."

If anything about this play reflects the mood that is spreading through Israeli life, it is that it is not a work with a thesis, nor a broadside, nor even a political drama. It represents something that has appeared suddenly among us, that is at hand, and that we are not frightened to examine. This is why Jagendorf sums it up very well. What is surprising about this work is not its sincerity, nor its honesty—it has both—but its "lack of hate."

To understand the existence of the other and then to admit his existence without hatred is something new in Israel, even though some democratic sectors have always lived this way. However widespread the mood is—even if it has not yet become a state of conscience—it is the first time it has ever happened.

A new reality is taking shape through dispersed links which can be found in the most unlikely places, but which are concatenating with each other. Unexpected attractions begin to operate, as if unleashed by a review of the consciences of the two peoples of this region who have committed such atrocities upon each other.

After surrendering to the Israeli Army, and still carrying the heavy load of six weeks of hiding in orange groves to elude Israeli patrols, the PLO commander of the Sidon region declared that he had reached a conclusion: that the era of armed struggle was over, and that Palestinians should now advance their cause in the political field.

At the age of thirty-nine, Assad Suleiman Abdel Khadel has eighteen years of war in his past, eighteen years of sacrifices, mistakes, and searching. He believes today—and I agree with him—that he was right in surrendering because, as he says, "Another death, whether Israeli or Palestinian, will not solve the problem. On the contrary, it will just make another family unhappy."

I believe Khadel when he says that "an entire people cannot be judged on the basis of a group which has committed damning acts of terrorism."

Rarely do we, the Palestinian and Israeli peoples, reach that culminating moment in the encounter of two enemies when they mutually confess their crimes, their terrors, and their inevitable need for each other.

8

The least I can do today is recall General Ariel Sharon's original battle plan: To drive the Palestinian guerrillas back, 40 kilometers behind Israel's northern frontier, in two or three days, no more than seventy-two hours.

This meant—the government said so—peace for Galilee. I remember this today as the seventh week of the war is closing, because, on the forty-fifth day of the invasion, Palestinian guerrillas are still operating on Lebanese territory occupied by the Israeli Army. A rocket fired from the area controlled by the Israelis hit a settlement in Galilee, and settlers had to scurry to the shelters. Today, too, Palestinian guerrillas ambushed an army patrol on Lebanese territory controlled by the Israeli Army, killing five of our soldiers.

As with so many things here in Israel, there is no consensus on these two events, despite their dramatic significance. Still, they affect our mood. The conclusions about the war that we draw up at the end of the day, even those reached from opposite points of view, envelop us in feelings of dejection and frustration.

Some of us believe these incidents resulted from the failure to liquidate the Palestinian terrorists holed up in Beirut. Others think they resulted from our failure to understand history, in not realizing that Palestinian terrorism against Israel will continue until the Palestinians have a country of their own, until Israel quits Palestinian land on the West Bank and Gaza to allow the creation of this Palestinian homeland.

It makes no sense to argue that the Palestinians fighting Israeli invaders in Lebanon are terrorists. Yet it's clear that even if we accept that they are terrorists, it is evident to all fair-minded Israelis who have not been terrorized by government propaganda that the military suppression of 10,000 guerrillas (or terrorists) who arose from the heart of a population of 4,000,000 Palestinians will give us at most a tenuous five-year interlude, until the next generation of guerrillas (or terrorists) is ready to resume the armed struggle. History tells us that the new wave of fighters will be more radical, better trained, and more desperate.

The two blows struck today against the euphoria of those who believed that all our problems had come to an end merge with the pessimism generated by the general conviction that there will be a change in our relationship with the United States. They also meld with reports of rebel action on the West Bank and Gaza, though the government had assured us that our triumphs in Lebanon not only meant peace for Galilee, but tranquillity and silence in Judea and Samaria.

A sensation of despair wells up and envelops even those of us who are opposed to military solutions, who are against recourse to violence. We are aware that we're still invincible, but not absolved, not untouchable. Our entire military capacity cannot stop a couple of Palestinian youths from making a bomb that will explode in Galilee, or from murdering an Israeli official in Bethlehem, or from ambushing an Israeli patrol in the middle of Lebanon. It's true, we're invincible, they can't defeat us, but neither do they disappear. We're not accustomed to this strange condition of vulnerable victors.

We realize, too, that our military strength, the result of our brains, dedication, and patriotism, is also a consequence of our association with the United States. The momentary halt of American supplies of cluster bombs does not make us believe we have lost the impunity we enjoyed; after all, our impunity was based on our being the only favored U.S. ally in the Middle East. Nothing indicating a substantial change in this relationship has yet occurred. But we are a people who too often in the past have had to anticipate the changes that will affect us. We have, in effect, become expert in sniffing out the evolution of history, though too many times we have remained paralyzed even after we reached the right conclusions.

Today the Israeli citizen reads and hears that nothing has changed in our relations with the United States, but he senses that his ally no longer feels inextricably tied to Israel. If this is indeed true, we must then forget about our impunity. What remains? After all this, it seems that what remains is the other, the eternal and immovable presence of the other, the irreducible Palestinian.

Nobody can escape the burden of what is happening to us. The discussions and disputes between friends, in the privacy of families, are considerably painful. All of us are emotionally unsettled every night by television reports announcing the names of our soldiers killed in action, their personal histories, their ages, averaging a little over twenty, and the details of their funerals.

When I try to make sense of what has happened and is happening, even in the most elementary fashion, I always reach the same end: the bare and unavoidable image of the other, the Palestinian.

I have often seen the victimizer reach the point of loathing his victim because of the effort he must make to continue hating. It's a strange phenomenon that makes elimination of the victim more gratifying and more necessary than the pleasure of punishing him.

Often I can't help feeling this way toward the Palestinian, whose very existence is living testimony to my hazardous survival in this part of the world, to the survival of all who surround me, of my own people. I'm not the only one troubled by these problems. We're all anguished by the magnitude the Palestinian presence has acquired during this war.

Many of us, surely a majority of the Israelis, want the Palestinians to vanish physically from this region, want them banished from our presence. Others dream of the possibility of a sudden miracle that will settle them happily and forever somewhere far from us. As if Palestinians could be rendered docile by a vanishing act, or happy through an act of magic.

Nothing assuages our anguish better than to repeat three long lists to ourselves:

The crimes of humanity against Jews.

The crimes of the Palestinians against Israelis.

The slurs of the anti-Semites who now have taken up the Palestinian cause to advance their lunatic interpretation of the Jewish presence in history and of the Jewish mystery.

Living in Israel, this little country that one can travel through so easily, passing the same places several times a year, one encounters everywhere the burning presence of Palestinian crimes. The children murdered in schools up north, the years spent in shelters, the deaths of civilians on fields and roads, in city theaters, in buses on the highways. This list of crimes must also include the political stupidity of the Palestinians, for it is a stupidity that has many times killed the efforts of Israelis who were seeking a peaceful solution to our conflict. On the list, too, is the murderous use to which Arab countries have put the Palestinian drama, with the sole object of eliminating both Israel and Palestine.

I would also place on the list of plain and simple murders, of wanton crimes against us and against the Palestinians, the obscenity of the anti-Semitism that the Third World's left tries to hide behind delirious political interpretations or barely disguised ritualistic formulas and symbols.

When I have finished drawing up all these lists, I weigh and reweigh them, I consider and reconsider them, and my will to survive as part of the Jewish people on this earth becomes stronger than ever; but once again the Palestinian emerges, each time with a stronger and more clearly defined outline. It is as if the tragedy which Lebanon, the West Bank, and Gaza are currently enduring had at long last finished his-

tory's painful effort to give birth to him. It is somewhat like
the birth of the political Jew, who became clearly defined
after the waves of anti-Semitism that shook an enlightened
France at the end of the nineteenth century. Like one of
those historic presences that are born when the inevitable
becomes unbearable, born through the power of necessity, as
the ancient Greeks said.

At the end of the seventh week of war we speak a language
different from that used in Israel's lightning wars. Now we
say: One more week, we'll see what the next one brings.
We're at the end of a week that, according to the government's first forecasts, should never have been. We already
know, with near certitude, what could be the most important
result of this war.

We were told that the PLO would be destroyed, that terrorism would disappear, that the inhabitants of the West
Bank and Gaza would submit passively to our authority, that
Lebanon would have a strong, stable, and democratic government allied to Israel, that a whole gamut of new political,
diplomatic, and strategic opportunities were opening up in
the Middle East for us and the United States, our ally.

Everything was singing victory.

We enter the eighth week. What remains? Certainly not
new opportunities in the region. We are barely participating
in the diplomatic moves and our ally has not changed its
relationship with the Arab world. Just as before the war,
America is striving to strengthen the same countries, seeking
new alliances, and its leaders know that in both pursuits what
they achieve will depend more upon their attitude toward
the Palestinian issue, toward the Palestinian people, than all
the military might Israel can deploy.

The new diplomatic and strategic opportunities are for the
Egyptians and the French. Egypt has returned to the Arab
world without breaking relations with Israel. Yet we were led
to believe that we had achieved a division among the Arabs.

France in turn returns to the Levant in the name of the democratic and progressive ideals its president stands for in Europe. Yet we were led to believe that the left would never again play a role in the Middle East because it was so engrossed with the Third World that it could not bother with the preservation of Israel.

As we enter the eighth week, what remains of all this? We, the Israelis, remain. They, the Palestinians, remain. After forty years, after several wars, after so many alliances and unutterable sufferings, so many political shifts, the protagonists remain the same, and we are still in the same place. We remain, Israelis as well as Palestinians, the same dying ones. The political boundaries have been altered several times, but basically both of us remain in the same place. We have denounced and insulted each other, we have murdered, persecuted, and beaten each other, but we remain the same, and we are stuck in the same place.

While Jean Daniel, in Paris, thinks he has discovered in Israel "a country like any other," the journalist Meg Greenfield, in Washington, sees the Israelis converted into real people, like the others. Some believe that as a community we have ceased to respond to a moral purpose.

Perhaps all this is true, but it cannot be the only truth. Even though day after day an ever-greater number of Israelis find consolation, justification for the ever-greater presence of the Palestinian tragedy, this is not true, it cannot be true.

It is comfortable to say that the war we have unleashed on Lebanon is less cruel than the one Iraq launched against Iran, or the United States against Vietnam, or the Soviet Union against Afghanistan. It is still more comforting to claim that our army behaves better than the South Africans in Namibia, the Ethiopians in Ogaden, the Vietnamese in Kampuchea, and the Syrians in Lebanon. It's almost pleasant to hear time and again that our military censorship is practically nonexistent when compared to that of the British during the Malvinas-Falklands conflict.

We're always better than the worst; or, put another way,

perhaps we're better than the best. But the moment that we accept this premise, we may well start to lose our Israeli permanence, our Jewish continuity.

The historical backwardness of the peoples of the region, particularly that of the Palestinians, obliges us to deal with the Arab countries from a moral standpoint. To profit from this moment in history, from this stage of development, which would be in keeping with the tradition of other nations, would compromise our future as an independent country.

Even though each Israeli citizen interprets this differently and reaches different conclusions, at some point, over some issue, we must eventually admit to ourselves that we cannot be like the others. In these terrible days it's not easy to accept the war; it's much easier to lapse like the others, led by comparisons with the worst or the best. But in moments of lucidity, when reality is purer, we know that, for several generations, we cannot be like the others.

In one of his visits to Beirut in the company of bodyguards and journalists, General Sharon stopped to watch a group of his soldiers on the warm and sandy Juniye beach. They had leaped out of their vehicles, vigorous, young, bearded, victorious. They ate broiled crawfish, drank fruit juices, and joked with the generous Lebanese Christian girls. The French journalist René Backman remarked in a column:

"And what if after leaving behind the desert battlefields, the Israeli soldier becomes a soldier like the others?"

It's believed in Beirut that after such a scene, even General Sharon began to worry. Israel cannot survive with an army like those of the others.

The logical consequences of becoming a state like all the rest are obvious. The corruption of the *dolce vita* in Lebanon's cities if the war becomes Vietnamized, extended, without a light at the end of the tunnel; division in Israel if the war becomes Vietnamized; disputes within the military, first in the ranks of the reservists, then the regulars. And then what?

I believe that even if this scenario should come to pass, at the end all that would remain, again, would be the presence of the other, the Palestinian. Once again the same people remain, in the same place, but in much more difficult conditions for everyone.

Israelis must somehow be convinced to accept these new Jews of the Middle East, these citizens of a land that's not a country, these Zionists with neither a Herzl nor a Ben-Gurion, these Palestinians who refuse to go away just as they refuse to renounce their country. Their crimes and mistakes are not proof that their historic claim is not right and just. If we could learn to accept their human identity, as we did with the Germans after World War II, we would know how to accept their national identity.

Despite all of our government's efforts, and all the efforts of the official propaganda machine, to hide the fact and to pretend the contrary, the Palestinians were preparing to recognize Israel before we invaded Lebanon. Even now, despite their present difficulties, they have signaled enough political openings, which should be seized by the Israeli government. We, as well as our American allies, should understand that once again Henry Kissinger was wrong in his assessment of the war in Lebanon. Contrary to what he said—and led the U.S. and Israeli governments to believe—this invasion has not opened up a vast array of opportunities for Jerusalem and Washington. What this war has demonstrated, and continues to demonstrate with today's sad news—once more the fighting is renewed and helicopters laden with the bodies of young soldiers are returning to Israel—is that only one new opportunity has emerged: the mutual recognition of the two peoples, Israeli and Palestinian. Neither the Machiavellian dealings of the Saudi Arabians, nor the careful strategy of the Soviet Union, nor the deployment of American diplomacy, nor the swaggering of Menachem Begin and Yasir Arafat can produce any other opportunity than another variation on the endless butchery. Peace is the only opportunity.

At times Israel dissolves before us and among us—we cannot recognize our youthful democratic nation in the news and images. Those telling us about our presence in Lebanon seem to respond more to their obsessions with the international press than to our questions and uncertainties. The concern over what will become of our people, what will become of the others in Lebanon, gives way to other priorities such as demonstrating our generosity as occupiers and proving that the international press hates us.

We have returned to the ghetto, to the mood that prevailed in the ghetto, where survival meant knowing that the other hated us, meant defeating the other. Why has Israel, which was created to forget the ghetto, recreated it? Amos Oz once pointed out that Begin's Israel was a prolonged act of reprisal against the world by the Jewish people. Is he settling an account?

And why is it that we have locked ourselves into a ghetto once again, waiting for the rich uncle from America to help us endure?

No doubt, Begin's personality has remained fixed by the challenges of the ghetto. A bitter critic of the entire political and social process that brought about the creation of Israel, as well as the way the country was governed in his thirty years of opposition, Begin goes backward in vindication of his past. If he carries along with him a certain ruling class, it is because he provides their parties, which are generally centrist and rightist, with their only chance of achieving power. If he carries a large popular following, although not an absolute majority, it is because he has become the answer to the strongest motivation of all reactionary populism: resentment and frustration, now also feeding on patriotic braggadocio.

There must be a way out of this absurdity, because it is impossible for us to remain trapped in the ghetto. I believe that today we need the Palestinians as much as they need us. Each can serve as the democratic spark to the other.

But once again it's reported that air, tank, and artillery attacks against Palestinians have resumed in West Beirut, and against Palestinians and Syrians in Mansura, Bar Elias, and Baalbek, on the road to Damascus. This is a war that has already gone on far too long; yet we know all too well how we'll spend tomorrow's wait.

First, there will be a couple of grievous hours while families are informed of the death at the front of one of their own. Then, at night, a television announcer will soberly tell us their names, ages, and place of burial. Perhaps we'll be fortunate and find that none of ours has been harmed. It's possible that nobody we know, no neighbor, no friend of a neighbor, has been touched. Or the son of somebody we had forgotten. Or somebody we met at a party. Or somebody about whom we read a poem. Or somebody whose girlfriend we know.

But such good fortune is unlikely in this small and under-populated country. When tourists praise us, they often re-mark that we seem like members of one family. This is no longer true. The intolerance and violence of the past few years have changed the fabric of our society. Once pluralis-tic, now it is no more than confused. Yet we know almost everybody, or know about each other, so misfortune and sorrow become something personal.

The loud arguments that broke out today outside Beit Sokolov, the Press Association's Tel Aviv building, had a per-sonal tone, too, which embarrassed foreigners in the crowd. "Soldiers against Silence" was holding a protest watch to demand the return of their comrades from the front. Passers-by began to stop and shout their opinions, whether for or against, at the top of their lungs, as is the custom here. Yelling from their seats, drivers stopped their cars to join in. Police trying to restore some order did not keep their two cents to themselves, either, and a couple of adolescents selling ice cream had their best day.

We are entering the eighth week of war, and the contro-versy over our virtues and defects has reached the point of alienation. For every Lebanese expressing satisfaction with the arrival of Israeli troops, there is another Lebanese who demands the withdrawal of Palestinians, Syrians, and Israelis;

and there is a Lebanese Christian who fears the Lebanese Muslims if the Israelis go, and a Lebanese Muslim or Druse who fears the Christians if the Israelis remain. We're immersed in this kind of lamentable confusion, one that acquires painful overtones when the controversy is shifted to comparing Israel's hospitals, where there is always a Palestinian whose life was saved by our doctors, with the ruins of Lebanon's hospitals, where little can be done for the wounded; or to the devastated Palestinian camps, which this winter will have to provide shelter for the 400,000 Palestinians remaining in Lebanon after the PLO's removal from West Beirut.

Finally, the controversy becomes pathetic, even macabre, when the Prime Minister—in answer to criticism of this needless war and the references to the three hundred killed in the first seven weeks of the war, who should never have perished—believes he can invoke the categorical argument of the six thousand Israelis who died in the War of Independence or the twenty-five hundred in the Yom Kippur War.

Amid the convolutions of this controversy, the Israeli must seek the elements of judgment that will allow him to understand the reality of what is taking place—without demagogy, without opportunism, and without appeals to our tragic collective memory.

We learned today that Shimon Peres, the Labor Party leader, is involved in intense negotiations to avoid a major Israeli Army attack to seize West Beirut. He will be accused of encouraging the PLO's political maneuvers once it is sure that Sharon's sword no longer hangs over its head. Yet at the end of the seventh week of war it is clear that the only way out of the quagmire is for the PLO to find a political solution, and an adequate guarantee for the security of the Palestinians who remain in Lebanon after the PLO's military withdrawal.

Even though Shimon Peres, as in the first week of war, still believes that he must wait until the end of the fighting to voice his criticism, his activities are just enough to raise the spirits of lucid or merely troubled Israelis. Even though what he is doing occurs in private, at least it is no secret that he considers the war a political error, believing that the military strategy was mistaken, that there is no military answer to the Palestinian problem, and that we can count on western Europe for a political solution with sufficient guarantees for Israel's security. He also foresees the coming electoral victory of the Labor Party. I agree with him that it will be the only chance to get Israel out of the ghetto into which Begin has locked us.

The official propaganda machine, of course, will contest the conviction of a Labor victory with statistics and public opinion polls. But by the time the next elections are held, the harsh demands of Israeli daily life will have replaced the fervor aroused by military victories.

In the first few weeks of the war, Israelis loved to watch their prime minister on television, joking with our rich uncles from America at some impressive banquet where the uncles arose from the table to leave us their checks. Everything for us. In those first weeks, we also watched the arrival of dozens of these uncles, all of them eager to dump their fortunes on this little country to supply our needs, regardless of how urgent or great they might be.

But today, the Friday of the seventh week, while we prepare the Sabbath family dinner, while our women make sure we have enough candles, while they determine whether the entire family will be together, whether friends will join us, we learn that we, the Israelis, will be the ones who will pay for the war. We also learn that apart from the inevitable increase in the cost of living, we will have to turn over to the government a larger percentage of our incomes until we have contributed $1 billion by April 1983. To be sure, a forced loan, but without any assurance that it will be the last, or that the billion dollars will be the only cost.

Official propaganda depicts us as a people enthusiastically undertaking the sacrifices we must make. It is true that we don't evade them, but we undertake them with considerable anxiety. In the seventh week of war, we are almost somber.

There is no magic in Begin's boasts. When my wife lights the Sabbath candles tonight, it is her privilege to open her heart to God, and her hopes have the privilege of being expressed.

I would ask for a Palestinian state to emerge from negotiations in which Shimon Peres would represent Israel, and in which he would fix the limits of our security. Before anything else, we need to guarantee Israel's security rather than, as Begin is endeavoring, to raise the walls of the Israel Ghetto.

In the past few weeks, these walls have been breached a number of times. By soldiers who come back from the front demanding an end to the war. By military judges who are sentencing dozens of soldiers charged with plunder and acts of extreme brutality. And by reporters who, like Benny Morris and David Bernstein, write prudently and soberly in the Jerusalem *Post:*

We have heard rumors of a widespread PLO protection racket—but our Israeli Army spokesman points out that the PLO had all the money it needed, and whatever isolated cases of extortion there may have been were probably intended as a show of strength.

Our overwhelming impression of life in southern Lebanon during the years of PLO rule, then, is that it was nasty and brutal, with fear never far below the surface—fear of the PLO's arbitrary rule of the gun and, in several cases, the even greater fear of Israeli air strikes and artillery barrages.

But it must be noted that apart from a few notorious massacres at the height of the 1975-76 Lebanese Civil War—in Tyre, Aishiye, and, most of all, Damour—we could find little or no substantive proof for many of the atrocity stories making the rounds.

But it's not enough to penetrate the walls of the ghetto. They must be destroyed, razed. Even if a small section remains standing, we would change from a ghetto state into a Spartan state. Neither of these should be Israel's destiny.

9

In the early days of the invasion, the Israeli Army officers who escorted me to Tyre and Sidon had believed it was imperative to withdraw from Lebanon within a few days and return to Israel, or, at least, withdraw from Beirut. In the eighth week, the experts still maintain that we are running out of time, and the government's unofficial spokesmen affirm the same, in dramatic tones: "Time is running out."

Yet nothing seems to have changed, except for more Lebanese, Palestinian, and Israeli deaths, more destruction, and more pain. It seems as if our lives in the Middle East unfold on several simultaneous ups and downs: we're always running over the same space, but always remain in the same place, even though everything is in motion.

We are being subjected to a barrage of odious comparisons, abusive similes, and ridiculous charges that have given inhuman proportions to our awesome tragedy. Begin has accused Arafat of being a Hitler, and Arafat, unable to find a more damning epithet, has called Begin a Hitler. Journalists and politicians are also corrupting words and symbols, confusing the issues. Then, when it appeared that at last some moderation was descending on the language of participants and observers, Leonid Brezhnev, chief of the world's second military power, lurches into the act and charges that Israel is guilty of genocide in Lebanon.

It would be ridiculous to seek a description of genocide in any dictionary or in the files of the United Nations. The Soviet leader used the word essentially for political ends. What makes his ploy so dangerous is that it will impede the precarious chances of avoiding a massacre in Beirut. Yet, to understand the enormity of Brezhnev's obscene accusation, simply consider this century's genocides. There have been killings and massacres differing in origin and kind, epoch and ideology. There were the Soviet Union's gulags between 1930 and 1960, and Chinese Communist detention camps between 1930 and 1950 and during Mao's Cultural Revolution. Leo Kuper, a scholar on genocide, remarks that during the last fifteen years we can count the massive killings in Indonesia in 1967, Burundi in 1972–73, Kampuchea in 1975–76, East Timor in 1975–76, Uganda in 1976–78, Argentina in 1976–80, the Central African Empire in 1978, and Equatorial Guinea in 1977–79. Missing from his list are Vietnam, Rwanda, Algeria, Sudan, South Africa, Afghanistan, Namibia, Eritrea, Ethiopia, Chile, and the killing of Indians in Brazil.

But when Brezhnev employs the word "genocide," we can only think of the 1,500,000 Armenians massacred by the Turks during World War I, which, chronologically, is considered the first true genocide of the twentieth century. Then there are the 20,000,000 Soviets of World War II as well as the 6,000,000 Jews, the 3,000,000 in Bangladesh, and 1,000,000 Ibos in Nigeria.

Israel is not guilty of genocide in Lebanon. I believe Israel will never commit genocide. Every lunatic accusation hurled at Israel does nothing to blunt the aggressive designs of some of our leaders because the charges can be easily scorned. But they do create problems for democratic Jews here, as well as in the Diaspora, who are convinced that our policy toward the Palestinians is cruel, unjust, and inhuman, and must be changed without delay. It is painful to interrupt our struggle to disclaim these absurd charges, the latest of them made by a power that should be playing a positive role in the pacification of the Middle East.

It is a shame that time and again we are the ones who must define the boundaries of the issues and the true outline of the conflict, a role that should be played by the democratic left in western Europe and Latin America, and by U.S. and Canadian liberals.

We're choking here on the huge hunks of history that have been forced upon us in recent weeks. Neither we nor the Palestinians have had time to digest the layers of new facts and perspectives, even though we don't do much more than tell ourselves that in the Middle East one stage has ended and another has begun. We assume that nothing will ever be what it was. We believe that if terrorism returns, it will be, in the eyes of the masses, shorn of its previous prestige and glory, marginal and factional. We also foresee that Israeli society must change. Yet there still exists a great confusion between the consequences of the war on the Israeli citizen and on the foundations of Israeli society.

The first consequence, a reduction in our standard of living, is already upon us. Emigration for economic reasons is possibly next. Another possibility is that all those who practiced self-censorship to avoid rocking the boat during the fighting will speak out when the soldiers come back from Lebanon, and their views will surely produce new political facts, which could bring a Labor government to power. As the history of this century demonstrates (the defeats of Woodrow Wilson after World War I and Winston Churchill after World War II being the obvious examples), this would almost be a natural consequence, yet it would not imply a substantial transformation of Israeli society.

At the beginning of the eighth week, nobody knows what to do. The Saudi Arabian and Syrian foreign ministers have returned to their countries from diplomatic trips. Philip Habib, the American mediator, has left Beirut to visit the region's capitals. A hundred initiatives have been discarded and just as many are under consideration, and still nobody knows what to do. But regardless of the solutions concocted by the diplomats, the consequences and changes will respond to what has happened until now.

If you drive along Israel's roads picking up representative hitchhikers one at a time, it takes no more than a couple of days to get the views of the various sectors of Israeli public opinion. There are many soldiers on the Tel Aviv–Haifa–Naharia–Rosh Hanikra highway, who, in civilian life, reside in cities along the way: Natanya, Hedera, Rosh Pina, Haifa, Acre, and Naharia. Many more civilians, especially from the farm settlements, are thumbing rides on the Hedera-Afula road. The number of troops increases between Afula and Tiberias, and beyond Tiberias almost everyone on the road is a soldier, heading north, to Safed, Rosh Pina, Kiriat Shmona, and Metulla, or to Ein Gev and Golan. Driving south, there are few soldiers on the way to Beersheva and Eilat on the Ashdod road. More soldiers than civilians are on the highway to Jerusalem, from where they enter the occupied West Bank territories.

I don't exactly converse with the hitchhikers; I simply listen to an endless outpouring of opinion. My ignorance of Hebrew is no problem. With Ashkenazis, we usually speak English, unless they are from Latin America or the children of Latin Americans who came twenty or thirty years ago. All those born in Israel understand the tongue of their parents. Occasionally I pick up Spanish Jews from Seville, Malaga, Barcelona, or Madrid. With Sephardis from Arab countries, we talk French. The Sephardis from Bulgaria, Turkey, and Greece speak Ladino, the fifteenth-century Spanish of their ancestors, which fits well with my twentieth-century Spanish.

In the city I also hear the opinions, of students, recent immigrants, and intellectuals, as well as items from Hebrew newspaper articles that are translated or explained to me.

All of us try to guess what our lives will be like from now

on. In the eighth week of the war, what surprises me most is the capacity of the Israelis to be astonished by the things that are happening to us. When the death of a soldier at the front is announced, the most usual reaction is: How is it possible that our people are still being killed? They adhere to a simple stereotype of our position in the region: We're the good and the mighty. Perhaps this explains why despite five recent wars affecting two or three generations, despite pacifist and dissident movements, there has been no real anti-war literature—no *All Quiet on the Western Front,* no *The Naked and the Dead.*

I think that one of the substantial changes in Israel will be the joining of the political pacifism born in the late 1970s with a political anti-militarism.

I believe there will spread a political anti-militarism that will combine forces with the political pacifism born in the late 1970s. It is entirely possible that the pride (expressed so often) that no draft card–burning movement like that of the young Americans who opposed the Vietnam War can thrive in Israel will be exchanged for pride in seeing Israeli youths demanding a peaceful settlement to the Palestinian issue as a way of seeking their generational demands: a shorter term of military service, jobs for young people, and the construction of homes for young married couples.

If Israel is shaken by Vietnamization of our youth, there will be a change no less important than the transformation in 1967 after the victory of the Six-Day War. At the time we spoke of "our Empire," inspired by a neurotic sense of national omnipotence. The change now could be equally profound, but in the opposite direction. It's possible that for the time being the idea of anti-militarism is too provocative, but the conversion is coming, even though it may adopt a different guise.

Another substantial change will spring from an overall reappraisal of what military power can achieve. Until this war, our might appeared unlimited; perhaps never before had we made such extraordinary gains. The lightning advance to Beirut was as spectacular as the military operations of the Six-Day War; but the paralyzed Arab nations did not intervene, the Third World failed to provide any sort of effective support for the Palestinians, and the Soviet Union was downright passive.

Yet if we add up all the triumphs of all the wars, including the present one, we'll understand that in order to achieve that definitive security we so anxiously desire, we shall have to go halfway down the road that separates us from the Palestinians. Even though we've defeated them militarily so many times, we have not gained any superiority over them. If superiority means security, we shall have to meet them halfway.

I'm convinced that this now burgeoning idea will be twisted by the militants to frighten the Israeli people. This has been their tactic up to now. They will declare that it is impossible to budge one millimeter from our position of force, that it is perilous to abandon our position of superiority because there is no acceptable peacemaker. Yet our might and superiority have not brought us peace, nor helped us achieve security. What good is power if it has been incapable of gaining these objectives? Strangely enough, it can be used to create a viable peacemaker. If someone who might negotiate refuses to do so because he is frightened by our power, we will be forced to employ our power to guarantee his security, without which we cannot guarantee our own.

I'm convinced that this will be a substantial change in our society. The conflict is between two peoples who are right, between two rights, between equal rights. This makes it a difficult conflict, but not one between enemies. Let me explain. It's true that peace is made between enemies, and many people maintain that, because we're enemies, peace can be achieved. Yet what keeps us fighting is not a war but a conflict over equal rights. A peace agreement won't be enough. We'll have to resolve the conflict over equal rights. And Israel has the strength to accomplish this.

In the eighth week of this endless war, the Israeli citizen has, to be sure, a right to a large share of pessimism. This time, however, the pessimism is corroding some deeply held notions on the management of the war and on our diplomatic strategy. Pessimism is also infecting the overall role that our military power should play in the Middle East. It's the sort of pessimism that is dangerous, because it's just one step from total skepticism and frustration. Israeli politicians and intellectuals must deflect it so that there can be the birth of a new hope, a new Israeli society. Nearly two millennia ago a Jew named Yehoshua (later known as Jesus Christ) tried without much success. But it seems to me that the prospects are better now, that more people are willing.

A major ingredient in the dangerous Israeli feeling of omnipotence was the unconditional support of Diaspora Jews for what they indiscriminately call Israel. Their few attempts to differentiate between country and government were too feeble to alter their ideas—or illusions—of Israel.

Menachem Begin's transgressions since he assumed power in 1977 have allowed a greater freedom of expression for those Diaspora Jews who believe that identification with Israel does not mean submission to its government. Yet Begin (and other Israeli officials and leaders before him) has always counted on the inevitable complicity of the citizenry.

This is understandable. The relationship between the Israeli citizen and the Diaspora is a difficult one. Israeli renunciation of the Diaspora, out of resentment that these Jews don't live in Israel, would mean that the Israeli would have to resign himself to the idea of a definitive, eternal, and solitary insertion into the Middle East, which is very frightening.

There are other resentments. The Diaspora is more pleasing to Jews who move in the world; for many Israelis the Diaspora has become more appealing than Israel. And there is still a subjective resentment: in the hearts of many Israelis who remain here, there are unconfessed moments of temptation for the life that can be enjoyed in the Diaspora.

This sometimes conscious, sometimes unconscious conflict becomes a sort of complicity among all those trying to extract from the Diaspora the greatest benefit for Israel. But, as usual, resentment makes nobody happy. With the invasion of Lebanon, our guilty conscience over the exploitation of the Diaspora emerged, and it turned visible, tangible. Many Israelis were offended—after all, it's not easy to face one's guilty conscience. But for many others it was a relief, a chance to unload the burden of resentment, to consider the Diaspora as a separate entity, as loyal Jews but not unconditional supporters. We discovered that, as always, one is better served by an ally than by a slave.

Sometimes a small incident can unleash a collective mood, or inspire an important popular psychological event. When the American senator Paul Tsongas declared in the plainest possible language that support for Israel did not imply support for Begin, he dispelled one of our popular obsessions. This notion was not evident in the first moments of the war. But when Tsongas spoke, after a group of U.S. senators met with Begin in Washington, his words conveyed great significance. Tsongas made it clear that our friendly relations with the United States were more important than our obligation to keep ourselves in a permanent state of war. In a country like ours, where citizens concentrate as much on the need of becoming better as on the demands of survival, where the people are so thin-skinned that they are upset by someone's remark that a table wine is not so good, Tsongas's implication that the perfect show of force we were making in Lebanon had not earned his support, because it was based on something much deeper, became the focal point of discussions as to how we can continue to be the principal American ally in the Middle East.

Because the idea came from a prominent U.S. senator with a record of friendship for Israel, it could not be discarded as can criticism reflecting anti-Semitic feelings and rebukes from the Jewish Diaspora. Given the wartime mood, criticism of the Lebanon invasion and its consequences by non-Jews can easily be presented to the people as an enemy concoction. It's much more difficult to evaluate criticism from Jewish personalities and institutions, although Israel's mass media do not report their views with any degree of enthusiasm. While the dissent of Jews abroad has been largely shrouded in Israel, there is a widespread feeling that their views are significant.

This tension between inside Jews and outside Jews will provoke still another important change among us. The alienating monologue we have held with the Diaspora will metamorphose into a real dialogue. They are beginning to want to be heard, and we are beginning to perceive that it will benefit us to listen. Up to now, the Israeli has hardly ever engaged in dialogue. There is little inside the country, and none with the outside world. If a dialogue does develop with Diaspora Jews who are loyal to their idea of Israel, with those who don't automatically ratify any policy of the Israeli government, then the Israeli's concept of reality will undergo a major transformation. Employment of dialogue as an instrument, as a system, will carry him quickly to a dialogue with the Palestinians. When the Jews of the Diaspora finally lose their fear of Israel, they will help us to abandon our fear of ourselves, and they will help us to emerge from our ghetto.

Only by living in Israel, immersed in the tangle of obsessions, phantoms, and terrors that affects our souls and deforms our ideas, can anyone understand what is surely incomprehensible for other peoples—that we have a free country. But we will not be truly liberated as a people until dialogue—talk—wipes us clean of the ghetto remnants we still carry within ourselves.

The solution to the Palestinian problem depends on dialogue, and it is clear that the chances that dialogue will become a part of Israeli life are greater now than before the war.

Yes, in the eighth week of war, the Israeli Air Force resumed bombing raids of Beirut, Israeli Navy ships lying off Beirut on the Mediterranean resumed their shelling, Israeli artillery resumed its barrages, and Palestinian and Syrian batteries resumed firing at our positions. The Syrian defense minister resumed his threats, which can only mean the use of a new generation of Soviet missiles against our cities. All this signifies only more of the same, death and destruction. Nothing is changed. Despite the temptation to journey to the front, I keep thinking of future changes in Israel, of a future and changes that seem very near. The new opportunities are really here, not on the battlefield.

It's hard for me to decide whether to return to Lebanon. It's not easy to swallow the government's efforts to prove our generosity as occupiers. Although there have been improvements in the situation of the Lebanese, introduced to the beat of massive publicity, the government will need a large dose of hypocrisy to convince me that we have brought happiness to Lebanon. Back in the third week of the war, General Sharon appointed an expert on rehabilitation and reconstruction to study Lebanon's needs. It was comforting to know that Arye Liova Eliav took on the job. He is a democratic leader involved in the struggle for a peace settlement with the Palestinians. He worked in Iran after the devastating 1962 earthquake, and in Nicaragua after the 1973 earthquake. In the seventh week of the war, nearly a month after he finished his survey and presented his plan of action, he has yet to receive a reply from the Minister of Defense. He says: "What is happening now is the worst possible situation. They are letting things take care of themselves without any planning or supervision, and allowing the classic dynamic of a refugee population to reestablish itself among the ruins, to assert itself.

"It is in Israel's interest—from a humanitarian, security, and political point of view—not to let this happen. Why allow a new sore to fester on the scars of the old?"

What more can I see in Lebanon that I did not observe on my first visit? True, things are better organized now. The battle for the conquest of world public opinion is rolling with a full head of steam. Journalists can have a good time there, escorted by officers trained in public relations and well informed of the weaknesses and eccentricities of their charges.

Perhaps they're right—or, to put it more precisely, partly right. A journalist in Beirut took 220 words to describe his lunch in an Israeli newspaper. He thoroughly enjoyed each mouthful and each word. He even included the brief text of the invitation he got from his escort: "Come and see Beirut burn, just like the emperor Nero."

But nobody received an equally generous invitation to visit the Palestinian camps. According to the official spokesman of our army, there are twenty thousand homeless people, not counting those in Beirut. According to Israelis like Eliav, who are striving to help the refugees, there must be between sixty and seventy thousand homeless people. David Shipler, reporting from Sidon, writes in the *New York Times:*

> . . . the Israeli army has made extraordinary efforts to keep the destruction out of public view by refusing to take visitors to the camps and trying to keep journalists out.
>
> Yaakov Levy, an official in the Foreign Ministry's information department, who was mobilized into the army's reserves to escort correspondents into southern Lebanon, said that any officer who allowed a reporter to see the camps would be placed in a military prison. Saying that Israel had to be spared bad publicity, he refused to permit a *New York Times* correspondent to visit Ein Khilwe, where many Palestinians are reported to have returned to live amid the rubble.

The fight to modify Israeli society will take place in Israel. I'm convinced that one of the results will be the decision of the Israeli people to reconstruct in Lebanon what our army has destroyed.

It will be one more way to allow us to establish a dialogue with the outside world. To renounce impunity, to take charge of what was destroyed, is a part of this dialogue. To ask the world's cooperation for the reconstruction we owe the world is another part of this dialogue. All reparation is an

act of civilization. That is what is expected of us, and it is
logical that it should be so.

I receive a clipping on Palestinian refugees from the Washington *Post:*

> The immediate answer to the plight of the refugees is for
> them to be sheltered and cared for under conditions
> posing no security threat to Lebanese or Israelis, wher-
> ever the space and facilities are available. Certainly they
> should not be hustled and hounded and deprived of shel-
> ter by Israeli soldiers. The middle-term answer is for a
> Lebanese government worthy of the name to take the
> responsibility of a sovereign state for all the people resid-
> ing in its territory. The long-term answer to the problem
> of the refugees, in Lebanon and elsewhere, lies in a
> political settlement that allows the camps—and the
> grievance and wound that they embody—to dry up.

Will there also be profound changes in Palestinian society?
We Israelis still refuse to believe their terminology, and they
refuse to become more explicit. But we, as well as they, know
that the Palestinians have accepted the existence of Israel
and its security.

The Palestinians have committed too many errors to make
these changes with ease. And there is no error more pathetic
than to yield the leadership of a liberation movement to a
terrorist. Something similar would have happened if Menachem Begin had liquidated Chaim Weizmann and David
Ben-Gurion.

It did not help the Palestinians to put themselves under
Hitler's protection through the Grand Mufti of Jerusalem.
Nor were they sustained by becoming at various times the
instrument or pretext of Nasser's ideological and geopolitical
fantasies, of Qadafi's, and now of Khomeini's. It did not serve
them to surrender to Saudi Arabia's diplomacy, whose only
objective is self-preservation. Nor to the alliance with Syria,
whose sole aim is to absorb eastern Lebanon and build a

Greater Syria. The Third World has offered nothing except to include them in their speeches and proclamations. And for the Soviet Union, they were merely a useful warehouse for obsolete arms in exchange for associating the Kremlin with Allah.

Nothing worthwhile resulted from this long series of illusions and efforts, which always ended in a massacre at the hands of the Jordanians, or of the Syrians, or of the Lebanese Christians, or of the Israelis. Nothing came of the large number of senseless murders of Israelis. Nothing was served by disguising the indifference or the hate of the Arab nations in the costume of solidarity. And nothing was served by cloaking the murder of Israelis in the religious texts of Allah or the ideological schemes of Marx and Ché Guevara.

A sterile diplomacy. A basic military capacity of almost no account. A terrorist strategy incapable of changing, even marginally, the relation of forces with Israel. And now, in Lebanon, the destruction of their homes, schools, farming cooperatives, industries, hospitals, and welfare organizations, and the waiting: for results from the political maneuvering of France, Egypt, Saudi Arabia, and the United States; for the pity of the world to provide some sort of sustenance for the 600,000 Palestinians who remain in Lebanon; and for a measure of dignity for the 1,250,000 Palestinians in the West Bank and Gaza.

How can anyone believe that there will not be substantial changes in Palestinian society? They will walk halfway down the road toward us.

This time, we must get out of the quagmire. I begin to count each day of the eighth week of the war. I know that I repeat myself, but I say to myself what I said in the third week: We can't go on like this; something has to happen.

The Israeli bombardments continue at the beginning of the eighth week. The number of victims among Palestinians and Syrians is not reported. An Israeli plane is shot down, its pilots taken prisoner by the Syrians. For two days now, a huge wave of rumors has made us fear the outbreak of a large-scale war with Syria. A member of Parliament, Amnon Rubinstein, worriedly asks the Prime Minister to authorize a separation of Israeli and Syrian forces along Lebanon's central and eastern fronts. Rubinstein assumes that this separation will avoid new encounters and will speed a solution to the situation in Lebanon.

But on the day Rubinstein formulates his appeal, the Prime Minister is concluding an agreement to bring the right-wing nationalist Tehiya Party, with its three deputies, into his government. Three is a number that can't be scorned, even though the party has opposed the Camp David accords in the Knesset, and clashed with the Israeli Army in the streets and buildings of Yamit to protest the return of the Sinai to Egypt.

The Tehiya obtained some rewards for its three deputies, even though I question their relevance to peace for the Israelis and the development of Israel—rewards that will become a heavy political and economic burden. In a signed agreement the government committed itself to constructing six thousand new homes and seven farming settlements in the occupied West Bank and Gaza. About $150 million will be invested in building an industrial infrastructure in the occupied territories, a project that will be managed by one of the three deputies from a new ministry that will be established for his personal use. The new minister, Professor Yuval Ne'eman, an eminent nuclear scientist, is convinced that Israeli territory encompasses the West Bank, Gaza, and southern Lebanon.

The incorporation of a minuscule political party, extremist and aggressive, into his government is our Prime Minister's idea of consensus and democracy.

10

Dozens of days without rain; hundreds of days will pass before it rains again. The Israelis have worked hard on this desert, and Tel Aviv is covered with gardens, flowers, and irrigation. But something is missing: that refreshing wave produced by a good rain. Every day, without letup, sun and dust, and the temperature at 85 degrees Fahrenheit. Every day, inevitably, the heat.

This year the heat arrived with the war. Now, after two months, both have the same flavor. They tire with repetition; they anguish with their inevitability. At the beginning of the ninth week of the war, during the first days of August, the heat seems eternal, so crushing and repetitive that it is impossible to suppose it will end one day. The war, too, repeats itself in such a way that it is not easy to imagine that some day it will end, that there can be days of heat without war, days without heat and without war.

To withstand the repeated, unrelieved heat requires establishing a method more subtle than resignation. To resign yourself to the Tel Aviv heat means to live clinging to the hope that it will stop at any moment. It doesn't help much to muffle the heat in a cape of silence, never mentioning it, and, in this way, never living it. Real veterans of these months of heat without rain that have gone on for so long without respite advise discussing the topic but without ever letting its true meaning appear, without ever saying it is horrible, awful, that Tel Aviv is unbearable in this heat and that one wishes to be somewhere else.

We're still not allowed to curse the heat in our city with the freedom of a New Yorker in New York or a Brazilian from Rio de Janeiro.

In the last week of the second month of the war, Beirut, an open city, has been bombarded by our army, navy, and air force with all the means at their command. We're told that terrorist emplacements and fortifications were attacked, that we had no casualties, and that all our planes returned to base.

The best way to withstand the heat is to talk about the war without getting to the bottom of the subject. Besides, who in this heat has the strength to meditate on the daily communiqués that are so easy to ignore? Who can devote himself to reconstructing the scenes, the details the government is trying to hide? The heat and dust of Beirut, the crumbling buildings, the lack of water, the wounded without hospitals, the dead without burial, and the desperate parents shattered by the guilt of being unable to protect their children, to hide them someplace, not see them mutilated.

Six days of bombardment. One bombardment lasts twelve hours, which the Lebanese daily *L'Orient–Le Jour* calls "Twelve Hours of Madness."

Many things have happened in the final seven days of last month and the beginning of this third month, but I remain fixed on these communiqués, so intelligently simplified that they can be digested in this constant heat, which has been the same for such a long time.

I remain voluntarily fixed on these communiqués, trying to see if their cynicism and the heat that overwhelms us justify the pragmatism of those who still cannot find reasons to feel morally deposed here in Israel, where what is moral has been the source of our devotion to the rebirth of the Jewish people.

The communiqués have served to report military operations and diplomatic negotiations. Not one dead person appears, not one demolished home. The word "enemy" is never used; the plans of those whom we have attacked with such effectiveness and success during the entire week are never mentioned, nor what are the real threats (if any) to us. In this vast haze, they are the terrorists, six to eight thousand in number, and we are left with the impression that each bomb hurled against Beirut lands on the head of some terrorist without ever affecting the daily routine of hundreds of thousands of the city's inhabitants.

Where have we found this capacity for cynicism?

Later, when we learn through the foreign press that between four hundred and five hundred civilians were killed in the bombing raids, we are told that the terrorists sought refuge among them.

Who gave us the right to decide that those civilians must die because they could not or did not know how to escape from the terrorists in time? Where did we get such omnipotence?

When the communiqués, in this week of heat and death, insist that the withdrawal of the PLO from Beirut and Lebanon will resolve the Lebanese crisis, and that the creation of a Palestinian state in Jordan will create the solution to the Palestinian problem, I think of Elias Freij, the moderate Palestinian mayor of Bethlehem. I recall some of his words, and I seek shelter behind them to protect myself from the official propaganda machine, which does not convince foreign correspondents but manipulates the fears of the Israelis, leading them to a pragmatic acceptance that civilians are dying in Beirut because they are guilty of a situation that has nothing to do with us.

Says Elias Freij: My roots are in Bethlehem. Here is my house. It was my father's, it was my grandfather's, it was my great-grandfather's.

Says Freij: Israel has the most formidable war machine in the Middle East. It will attempt to impose its solutions on the

peoples of the region, transform Lebanon into a protectorate. But we Palestinians are five million throughout the
world. We're hardworking and intelligent. We'll go forward.

Who has granted to the Israelis the Machiavellianism
needed to hide, with pragmatism, communiqués, and bombs,
these words of Freij's which invite dialogue and reflection?

The officers of the Israeli Army are young but not impul-
sive. In war, they're audacious but they don't improvise.
Every one of them can speak of heroic acts, for despite their
youth they have already experienced a couple of wars and
dozens of battles and operations. Yet they are modest. They
talk with great spontaneity, but never reveal the details of
their activities. They are great readers, true devourers of
books and magazines. They have a passion, an unquenchable
one, for specialized studies, for university courses, for semesters in which they can perfect their knowledge of computer
science or Greek history, French politics or the verses of the
Bible, modern mathematics or Phoenician voyages in the
Mediterranean. Some of them spend three months at Harvard or six months at Hebrew University or study a course at
Padua, the Sorbonne, or Oxford. Yet they never speak of
their fallen comrades and never give much thought to their
own fate.

It's easy to admire young Israeli officers, to wish them all
the best that's possible; to imagine them happy in their sober
habits, in their serious dedication to the army. It is an impressive list of virtues. Excellent qualifications with which to face
not only the danger of war but also the complexity of the
Middle East's political life.

Yet in these two months of Lebanization, many of them
(though not yet enough) have discovered that they have not
been trained for moments of doubt. They lack that important
and positive human dimension which is the capacity to
doubt, at some moment, everything, or nearly everything, or
at least of some aspect of everything. They have discovered
that if by some circumstance doubt sometimes assails them,
they are not prepared to devote the energy necessary to turn

doubt into action, which is, perhaps, the most human of all actions.

On the last Friday of the last week of the second month of the war, Israel's largest newspaper, *Yediot Ahronot*, devoted nine articles—a total column length of 962 centimeters—to Eli Geva, who at thirty-two is the youngest, most brilliant, boldest, bravest, and most likable colonel in the Israeli Army. And the first leader of such a rank and level, with such a military record, to convert his doubt into action.

In the last week of the second month of the longest war since the creation of Israel, he established in Israeli military tradition the possibility of doubt, the realization of doubt, and the risks of doubt.

Besides cutting through the nebulous official communiqués—trying not to become an accomplice because of the burden of fear incited among us, because of the burden of the routine, the heat and the weariness; trying to preserve a morality—this week the true significance of the doubts of Colonel Eli Geva had to be rescued from all the cynicism, prejudice, and tergiversation that the government set loose upon the Israelis just as it simultaneously and needlessly set the bombers loose upon the people of Beirut.

The facts are not very complicated: Colonel Geva commanded the first armored brigade to arrive in Beirut. He positioned his forces, organized his lines of defense, supply and communication, the evacuation and care of the wounded, the receiving point for instructions, and the analysis of the war's progress. He visited the families of his dead soldiers. He scrupulously attended to his staff officers, meeting for orders and explanations. He transmitted the orders he received, the descriptions of the political situation, and he knew how to report with humor the stories circulating in headquarters, the gossip, the anecdotes. It could even be thought that he had been born into this sort of life, his father being an army general and his brothers, like him, officers— although not exactly like him, because, as everybody agrees, he was unique, the best officer of them all. He went to the advance outposts and carefully observed the movements of the others through the streets of West Beirut. With his binoculars he stopped at every house, even at every window, every face in West Beirut.

As the days passed, in his land, in Israel, as well as here, at the front, the reasons he had for looking at that city and for trying to find out where his tanks should burst through into Beirut once he received the order to move forward no longer seemed so clear. The reasons were vanishing more and more swiftly day by day. Then he began to discover from his colonel's post—the youngest, the most admired—with his colonel's binoculars, faces and places he had not glimpsed before, but which also formed part of Beirut. When an armed Palestinian group appeared in his binoculars, he tried to follow all of its movements without distraction, without seeing anything other than the enemy, the terrorist. Then he noticed that this group was passing a group of children. He fixed his binoculars on the children. The next time he trained them for a longer period on some children playing on a street. The third time he followed some other children until they went into a school. The days passed, and each time West Beirut appeared more like a city peopled by children.

What happens to the children when a column of Israeli tanks, modern and of great firepower, manned by brave veterans, enters a city?

When Prime Minister Begin tried to convince Colonel Geva to withdraw his petition to be relieved of command, he was rejecting in a single gesture the doubts of the young colonel, his fears that the seizure of Beirut, the continual bombardment, would mean a massacre of the children. He said to Colonel Geva: "Did you receive an order to kill those children? So what are you complaining about?"

We must struggle in Israel against this kind of cynicism. We feel drunk with pride because our officers don't receive such orders. Let's go beyond that: because we know that our army does not aspire to kill children. Overcome by this obvious proof of morality and high principle, we forget the essence of Colonel Geva's message: that children die in war. Overjoyed because our Prime Minister never ordered the slaying of children, we forget to ask how many children were killed by Israeli bullets in Lebanon and why they died. Which is precisely what is at the bottom of the doubts of Colonel Geva, to whom it would be foolish to reply that Jewish children have died at the hands of Palestinian terrorists in Galilee, Kiriat Shmona, Maalot, Misgav Am, as they tell us, because he knows the figures and could respond that in the second month of the war more children were killed in Beirut than during thirty years of terrorism in Israel.

We Israelis are a brave and united people, yearning to live in peace. What dreadful conscious or unconscious elaboration of fear have they instilled in us that the majority accepts this coexistence with cynicism, so much complicity with cynicism?

Colonel Geva saw the faces of the children in Beirut, and he knew what awaited them if his tanks entered those streets, if his brave and efficient men raced through those streets and broke into those houses. The colonel also knew that the death of those children was not justified, politically or militarily, by the PLO's presence in Beirut. He knew that that presence did not have the importance official propaganda assigned to it. Even when the irresponsibility of the PLO kept the terrorists in Beirut, the death of the children was not justified. Even when Begin, in not assuming any responsibility for those deaths, seemed to be passing the burden on to God or to fate.

But there were still other faces that the colonel saw. And other deaths. When he reviewed his lines, his brigade's posts, there were the faces of his men. When he addressed them, he could look them in the eye, he knew their names, their backgrounds, professions, and families. He knew they could be killed if they entered Beirut, as General Sharon wanted, but he had to guess who would be killed. It was as if he had to decide these deaths, imagine them. And then, in his limitless anguish, he imagined the moment in which he would visit parents or wives to report these deaths, without being able to add, as he had at other times, that they had given their lives for the homeland. The colonel could not deceive himself about this: these lives would be offered to an absurd reading of reality by an ambitious Minister of Defense and a fanatic and possessed Prime Minister.

Colonel Geva would have to lie to those parents and wives, brothers and sisters, as he was lying now to his men with his silence, as he was lying to those children of Beirut, whom, according to his maps and information, he had to continue considering a military objective.

He asked to be relieved. The lives of his father, his brothers, his family, his own, had been spent in the army. He asked to be relieved and withstood the pressures—cordial, cynical, amiable—of his chiefs, and the arguments—cynical, lying— of his Minister of Defense, of his Prime Minister.

Colonel Geva emerged gracefully from the test; he defended himself well. Now we Israelis must defend ourselves. In the last week of the second month of Lebanon's invasion, the week of the most terrible bombing of Beirut, we must defend ourselves from the official communiqués and uncover what they hide. Defend ourselves from the accusations and interpretations provoked by the most heroic act undertaken by Colonel Eli Geva in his remarkable military career.

I don't believe he has demoralized the army. True, General Sharon won't be able to understand him; but Colonel Geva has given a new dimension to the Israeli Army. If we look to the future, we can see clearly that he has established a safeguard against the tendency to Prussianism that Prime Minister Begin has impressed on our army. Thanks to Colonel Geva we surely will be able to stop our officers from shielding themselves behind the classic formula, "I followed orders from above," and thus evade all responsibility for their actions, whatever they may be.

I don't believe that Geva has abandoned his men. He offered to give up his rank and serve with them as an ordinary soldier, to go with them to possible death and to become a murderer if they received the order to take West Beirut by assault. But his morality did not allow him to be the one who would lead them to death and crime. It is a shame that this act of love for his soldiers has not become an obligatory topic of discussion for teachers and pupils in Israel's schools.

Geva was relieved of his command, but his offer to serve as an ordinary soldier was rejected.

The government could not stop repeating what pride it felt for an army in which a colonel could make such a beautiful gesture. We would feel a greater pride if his gesture had indeed been understood, if an intense and open debate had been permitted. It's true that the issue has not been forbidden; soldiers and officers these days are talking about Colonel Geva. But this does not yet make us rely on the sort of army that the Jewish state should have. Our army should have organized lectures, talks, seminars, and discussions on Colonel Eli Geva's act of courage and sacrifice.

In 1948, shortly before the birth of Israel, a young Haganah settler on the plains of Sharon, halfway between Haifa and Tel Aviv, received an order from the Jewish underground army to seize a valley in Arab hands the very moment that the new state was proclaimed. The settler studied the environs of the valley, made plans, received the precarious and illegal military training of that time, avoided the British, and tried to remember the rudimentary books on strategy he had read. Then, all of a sudden, a Russian Jew arrived in his kibbutz: through the British blockade, through the frightful networks of the European displaced persons camps, a Russian Jew who had been a Soviet colonel in World War II.

Does anyone recall the prestige of the Red Army in the postwar years? You can imagine the long hours that the young settler, now confident and enthusiastic, spent talking to the colonel, drinking in his words, making notes, torturing successive interpreters. One day, with all due precaution, they went to survey the valley; then again, another day, and perhaps a third time. The colonel's judgment was positive. The valley could be taken. Two divisions were required, two well-equipped divisions. The settler was upset: he had been counting on forty young men from neighboring settlements. Some had machine guns.

Israel was proclaimed a nation and the valley was seized. Thus was formed the Israeli Defense Army. That army would have explored the meanings of Colonel Geva's gesture. Not prohibiting the discussions that soldiers and officers hold spontaneously is not the same thing as promoting a debate, analyzing an issue, and drawing public conclusions.

These days we must defend ourselves from simplistic— which I believe to be cynical—statements intended to make us feel more pride for our army than for Colonel Geva. We must strive to fix our hope on the possibility of an army that will assume the doubts posed by Colonel Geva, not on an army that has no room for Colonel Geva in its ranks.

He lives relatively near my house. I am on the northern edge of Tel Aviv, and some 20 kilometers further north is the town of Raanana. I already know that Colonel Geva cannot tell me anything new, and I don't think it necessary to bother him just to unravel small tales and secrets about what occurred. The essentials have already been said and done. True, he wasn't permitted to bid farewell to his men, but we can imagine what he would have told them. His message was clear enough.

At any rate, I go to Raanana to walk in front of his house, the typical dwelling of an Israeli officer. I stop at the corner. I wander through different streets and cover almost the entire length of the long avenue which, beginning at the highway, divides the town in two. It's an avenue of beautiful trees, filled with movement and businesses, and almost at the end is a shopping center with a charming café and an exuberant flower and plant store.

Raanana has grown rapidly in the last few years, being largely inhabited by young couples. New immigrants from South Africa and Argentina have settled in this pleasant town.

I'm not the only one staring at Colonel Geva's house. Like

the others, I pass by so as not to disturb him, but, like the others, I do it slowly and with my eyes on the house.

I'm convinced it's not curiosity that has brought me here. And if it is a feeling of solidarity, I have no means of expressing it. But it could be a need to confirm, to perceive the material forms, those that endow specific existence to an event I regard as historic.

It is possible that I have gone to Raanana just to feel once again that breath of fresh air in this long, hot, and implacable summer, in this long war, without objective and without pity, that Colonel Eli Geva's manly and mature act has unleashed.

In the streets of Raanana I repeat to myself some lines from *Israel 1969*, a poem that Jorge Luis Borges dedicated to Israel. It is one of the many poems in which the writer thinks of his possible Jewish ancestors and expresses his love for Israel. They are lines that could describe Colonel Eli Geva today, and perhaps many others, too, who have undertaken different forms of the struggle, have arrived here, and succeeded even in forgetting their nostalgia:

> *Forget who you have been.*
> *Forget the man you were in those countries*
> *which gave you their mornings and evenings*
> *and to which you must not look back in yearning.*
> *You will forget your father's tongue*
> *and learn the tongue of Paradise.*
> *You shall be an Israeli, a soldier.*
> *You shall build a country on wasteland,*
> *making it rise out of deserts.*

Borges understood that we Israelis are a people of lean beings, of forgetfulness, of a past without nostalgia. A people of soldiers who fight marshes and deserts.

In the streets of Raanana, Colonel Eli Geva's town, I think about these themes, walking beneath its trees and on the pathways of its parks. And I reach the point of believing that we are as Borges thought of us, or dreamed with his blind eyes and his beloved face lifted toward heaven while he walked with me through the streets of Buenos Aires, supported by my arm and his cane.

On my return to Tel Aviv I am informed that the army's chief rabbi, General Gad Navon, is distributing a map on which Lebanon is marked as the territory that was occupied in antiquity by the Israelite tribe of Asher. The city of Beirut has been Hebraized, appearing as "Be'erot."

The Israelis of Rabbi Gad Navon are not those of Borges. The soldiers of the chief rabbi are building a homeland by taking territory from others with arms, not building it out of marshes and deserts like the Israeli soldiers of Jorge Luis Borges, who in *To Israel* also believed himself to be a Jew when he asked:

> *Who can say if you are in the lost*
> *labyrinth of the age-old rivers*
> *of my blood, Israel? Who can say*
> *what lands your blood and my blood have roamed?*

The war of two or three days has now reached its fifty-eighth day. How many things must I have forgotten during this long war? A letter reaches me today to remind me that Ida Nudel is alone and ill in Moscow. In all this time, her name has been erased from my memory. Busy with the heroism of our soldiers, a heroism that some day we must analyze in the light of our impressive superiority in technology and weapons, we Israelis have forgotten other battles and other heroes, other battlefields.

The letter is from Elena Friedman, Ida Nudel's sister. Sweet Ida has concluded her captivity in Siberia, but the authorities in Moscow are continuing their campaign against this prisoner of conscience. She can't enter a hospital for adequate treatment of her cardiac condition.

As so often happens in this country—all too often, in fact

—we Israelis forget the Jews. Sometimes I seem to find a certain disdain for Jews on the part of Israelis. Her sister's letter reminds me that for almost a year I have done nothing for Ida Nudel: "Dear Mr. Timerman, I am deeply moved and encouraged by your continued concern and activity on behalf of my sister, Ida Nudel, as most recently expressed in your letter of August 1981." One year ago.

The Jewish Diaspora is here again. Its heroes, Ida Nudel, Anatol Shcharansky, are not celebrated and welcomed like the young Israeli tank soldiers who are shelling Beirut. Apparently concern for their problems, when compared to the desire, the irrepressible temptation, to seize the occupied territories and southern Beirut, can be postponed. Yet as we enter the third month of war, it is they, more than we, the Israelis, who represent the moral continuity of our people; they are the ones who uphold the principles on which this nation was founded. Their struggle for the right to dissent and national identity in the Soviet Union shows Israelis a better way to the solution of the Palestinian problem than Sharon's tanks.

These heroes don't ask for much. I could review once again the list of diplomats, politicians, and journalists I have turned to for help to assure Ida Nudel's right to join her sister in Israel. She asks much less. I write because in her solitude the letters she receives from abroad both sustain her and give a warning to the Soviet government. Anyone can write Ida Nudel at Yumikh Lenintzev No. 79, CPR P. 6, Apt. 28, Moscow, U.S.S.R.

And what if our priority isn't Lebanon? If our priority is the national Jewish identity in the Diaspora, or anti-Semitism disguised as anti-Zionism? Or anti-Semitism masked as denial of the Holocaust? Or undisguised anti-Semitism? Wouldn't we be confusing our priorities to promote an a-Jewish concept of our reality in the Middle East?

Not long ago, we who are hailed as the champion defenders of the existence of peoples, denouncers of all genocides, were capable of sabotaging the International Conference on the Holocaust and Genocide held last June in Tel Aviv, just before the war began. It seems centuries ago. We committed the sin of silence before the genocide of another people, just as we were sinned against in the 1930s and 1940s. We allowed threats to neutralize our morality, the message of our religious tradition, and we placed our silence and our intrigues at the service of a terrible crime. We who send young Israelis to their death in pursuit of conquest, who, for a geopolitical conception of our government, destroy lives and cities in another country, consider that we have the right to wash our hands of a terrible foreign drama to preserve, with our silence, the security of a Jewish community in Turkey threatened by its government. This is precisely what we fling in the faces of those cowards who remained silent about our drama in Germany in the 1930s so as not to risk their own skins.

These final days of the second month of the war are particularly terrible because all the moral doubt, the moral anguish, is reappearing in different forms. The doubts of soldiers and officers at the front, the doubts awakened in me about our Jewish sincerity by the forgotten drama of Ida Nudel, and the doubts about our human sincerity engendered in me by the case of the silenced genocide.

Mrs. Lenny Fortas, a participant in the conference along with twenty-five other delegates from Israel, the United States, Holland, and Canada issues a joint letter:

"The declaration of the establishment of the State of Israel states that . . . the State of Israel will guarantee freedom of religion, conscience, language, education and culture. . . .

"The International Conference on the Holocaust and Genocide, towards an understanding, intervention and prevention of genocide, was planned by a group of dedicated people, very much in the spirit of the above-mentioned declaration. The planning has been under way for some three years, during which the Turkish government became aware of the fact that the Armenian genocide would be discussed.

"It was with a shock of disbelief and incredulity that we

were informed that the Israeli government had succumbed to Turkish pressures not to support nor officially recognize this conference. Moreover, that the Israeli government has influenced many internationally well-known authorities, connected through their work with the study of the Holocaust, not to participate.

"The undersigned are shocked, saddened and very concerned about this development; it reminds us of the conspiracy of silence which helped to bring about the Holocaust in the first place. It is a development which is directly contradictory to the very essence of the existence of the State of Israel."

I conclude, then, that there are enough human beings among us for a new point of departure, to start anew from a second dream.

These are such terrible days of heat, defamation, obscurantism, and death that we have to return once again to the understanding that these brave, solitary figures disposed once more to fight all the battles (which Jews have always known how to do) will reintegrate the true essence of the existence of Israel.

We should feel comforted by the discovery of these brave individuals amid our people, as well as among those who are disposed to respect our identity and existence and live together with us.

I think of the French historian Pierre Vidal-Naquet, who, in France, is disputing the invasion of Lebanon, struggling also against the neo-Nazis' attempts to rewrite the history of their crimes against history, and against the Polish military dictatorship, demanding freedom for the Solidarity leaders, Lech Walesa, Edmund Baluka, Jacek Kuron, and all the other political prisoners in Poland.

Vidal-Naquet stands where we Jews have always stood: with all the just causes at once, with a humanist simultaneity of priorities.

And I think of the Roman Catholic bishop of demolished Tyre. The courageous Monsignor Haddad, who was celebrated by the Israeli press in the first days of Lebanon's occupation for his readiness to cooperate in the solution of his city's problems, has not become, as our government may have expected, a passive collaborator. For this reason, I am certain that in the future he will be a proud and vigorous actor in the establishment of peace in the region.

After eight weeks of official statements from Jerusalem on our kindness as occupants and on our dedication to the reconstruction of Tyre, Monsignor Haddad remarks:

"The arbitrary arrests constitute an insuperable barrier to the establishment of a just peace, which, the Israelis affirm, they desire to establish between our two countries. I have written to General Sharon about this, to demand that he take a courageous decision, but I have the impression that I have not been heard. The Israelis have done us a service in ridding us of the thousand and one states which were poisoning our existence, but they have not been able to establish a relationship of trust and friendship with us. At the beginning of the invasion, Mr. Meridor, in charge of economic matters, visited us and he was well received. Should he return now, everybody would turn their backs on him. People here are more than pained by the behavior of the Israelis.

"In all conscience, we cannot accept the criteria on which the arrests are made. We cannot admit that a person whose name has been found in some office of the Palestinian organizations should be treated as a terrorist. Only those who turn out to be guilty of precise crimes can be considered as such. The sympathizers of the Palestinian cause acted out of either conviction or necessity. The conditions which existed at the time must be taken into account. I am certain that 95 percent —if not 99 percent—of the people arrested are innocent."

The Israeli Army is acquiring stoves and winter clothing. Winters are harsh in Lebanon, especially in the villages and small towns which do not lie, like the large cities, along the coast. We already knew our occupation would be long, beyond the coming winter, but the news has the terrible power of the banal. Every Israeli knows personally many who will remain in that region with nothing else to do but endure the cold, miss their families, run risks, and guard with their weapons a situation that we will never fully comprehend. Our soldiers and our arms will have to indicate, from among all the groups that will try to exterminate each other, who will be the victims and who the victimizers. This time others will play the role of Kapos, the Jewish prisoners who worked with the Nazis.

In October, the weather will change in Tel Aviv. It's possible that in Lebanon they'll begin to feel the cold toward the end of September. Right now the heat is awful both here and there. When I was in Tyre, there was no electricity; my military escort allowed me to drink only bottled mineral water. It was dangerous to consume tap water, driven by portable generators. We had to travel north, to Sidon, to find something cold to drink. Sidon had electricity. Now we all have it: Tel Aviv, Tyre, Sidon, and some zones of Beirut.

One dwells on these things because of the persistent heat. And there is a tradition of being careful with water in cities that are surrounded by deserts or built on deserts. When we travel, we carry receptacles filled with fresh water in our cars, and take canteens if we are making long trips to the beach or out of the city. Each of our soldiers has two or three canteens. Israeli schoolchildren take along small ones when they go on field trips with their teachers.

We are always thinking of water. For this reason the government's communiqués, in these days of heat, announcing the frequent suspension of water supplies to West Beirut inspire sad reflections. It's true that the U.S. ambassador to the United Nations, Mrs. Jeane Kirkpatrick, like General Sharon, thinks only of the seven thousand terrorists in West Beirut; but with or without supplies, they were never a threat to the Israeli Army, and neither thirst nor hunger will decide their actions.

Yet we know there are a half-million persons in West Beirut, and we know that in these terrible days of heat they need water and food. We know that in winter, food is more necessary than in summer.

It is becoming difficult for us Israelis to take on the burden of this siege by our army. Against Beirut, says our government. Against seven thousand terrorists, says Mrs. Kirkpatrick. Against half a million people, in reality.

When I imagine the moments of thirst of Beirut's inhabitants—and here we know quite well what thirst can be and what it means, for we are trained to make sure that in summer our children drink water constantly—when I imagine those moments of thirst, I also imagine redeeming scenes. A group of thirsty Palestinian children approach an Israeli patrol, and our soldiers offer their canteens. They debate a little while among themselves, but they give away most of the canteens, keeping only one for the road back. The soldiers know nobody should be left without water.

I imagine another scene. At a siege control point, young Palestinians attempt to smuggle small containers of water in ambulances, pretending they are carrying wounded to a hospital. The Israeli officer in charge lets himself be convinced that they are carrying what they say, lets himself be fooled.

What else can be done in this infernal oven that is Tel Aviv? We sign petitions, we collect money, we demonstrate on the streets, we support politicians who have not allowed themselves to be drawn into the shameful nationalistic paranoia.

And I think, one more time, that out of so much pain, our own and that of others, important changes must emerge.

They are still bringing wounded Israeli soldiers from the north. They bring them to our hospitals in helicopters. Usually they are between eighteen and thirty years old. We know that the wounded in Beirut can't count on doctors, and that the few doctors now have no instruments, no medicines, and very few hospitals. And the few hospitals still working have no lights. And if they have lights, they have no water. But they have our bombs and shells, approaching them on every side.

We are surrounded by our pain and the frightful misery and desperation of the others.

The Labor Party leader, Shimon Peres, has demanded that

Israel halt the bombardment of Beirut. The bombs are mightier than his voice.

Beirut, martyr city.

What else can I call it? All comparisons arouse waves of protest. Serious and responsible voices remonstrate that it is not the Beirut–Warsaw Ghetto, nor Beirut–bombed London, nor Beirut–bombed Rotterdam, nor Beirut–heroic Stalingrad, nor Beirut–massacred Oradour, nor Beirut–massacred Lidice, nor Beirut–Republican Madrid.

I. F. Stone, the American journalist, compared West Beirut to Tel Aviv 1947. In 1947, the terrorist Menachem Begin blew up the British officers' club, killing thirteen persons. Begin's terrorists hid among the civilians of Tel Aviv. The city was sealed off for five days and the entry of supplies was forbidden, but water and electricity were not suspended. Begin's terrorists cached their weapons and grenades in schools, synagogues, under the beds of children. When a British patrol arrived unexpectedly at the home of a friend of mine who was a member of a terrorist group, he hid his pistol under the skirt of his aged grandmother.

Perhaps Stone is correct. We should not find similarities or symbols beyond our own drama. We should ask of all who from abroad, outside this region, are struggling for peace in the Middle East, that they abstain from inventing slogans for us. Right here is everything we need. It will do us good to learn the parallelism of our drama with that of the Palestinians.

Beirut–Tel Aviv 1947.

Beirut–Beirut.

Beirut–Martyr City.

Rage and Hope

Today, August 5, 1982, the government announces that nineteen soldiers were killed in a war that does not officially exist, in the battles to occupy West Beirut, in an invasion that does not officially exist.

Today is Thursday. June 5, 1982—two months ago—was a Saturday in which I was able to watch thousands of reservists crossing Tel Aviv to reach staging points before proceeding to the north. One of the songs heard that night told of those days of war when all that can be seen are soldiers going and coming, going to the front and coming from the front; but—says the song—there's always someone who doesn't return. This morning, as the ninth week of the war is ending, we learn that nineteen more will not return. The government assures us that their families have been informed. This way, those who have sons, husbands, or brothers in Beirut, and were not told experience an uncontrollable sensation of relief and joy. Later, a sort of feeling of guilt for the dead follows. Finally, the waiting begins anew, for the entry of troops into West Beirut continues, although, officially, we are not going to seize Beirut.

Last night our Prime Minister appeared on television addressing an audience of Diaspora Jews in the Chagall Hall of the Knesset. If he already knew about the nineteen fallen youths, he did not refer to them. Seldom is his vision of events based on immediate reality. This could be why he feels so comfortable with the Diaspora Jews, whose only objective is to raise money for Israel—they believe that this benefits Israel—and to shut their mouths. Not to ask questions, much less give opinions. These Jews, like Begin, feel more comfortable with the remembrance of what happened than with what is happening now.

I studied the gestures, the looks, the tilting of the head, the vocal changes, the silences, and pauses of our Prime Minister as he addressed his Jews last night. It is my belief that he is unbalanced.

I was alone in the room and I was startled a number of times. Later I recalled that madness arouses in others very deep fears which are buried in our psyche. I thought I should consult the Israeli legislation and determine whether a citizen can file an insanity suit against another. In Argentina, where it is obligatory to take cases of dangerous madness to the courts, twenty-five years ago a friend of mine filed an insanity suit against a Catholic priest who was the country's chief anti-Semitic propagandist. My friend's evidence to a Buenos Aires judge consisted of the charges that the priest formulated against Jews, and my friend argued that they were not political or ideological expressions but sheer madness. If the accusations against Jews were not declared insane, any Argentine could begin killing Jews in the belief that they were destroying the country, corrupting its women, and enslaving its men.

While observing Begin, I thought of the priest. Wasn't it the obligation of Israeli psychiatrists to demand an investigation? Isn't a prime minister who finds reasons for acting today against the crimes committed by the Nazis forty years ago acting on the basis of hallucinations clearly studied and described by medical science?

Even in his speech last night, the Prime Minister resorted to the powerful fare of 1,500,000 Jewish children murdered by the Nazis. The Diaspora Jews turned very sad, their unquestioning hearts in the throes of anguish. But if our Prime Minister had spoken of the nineteen young Israelis—they, too, were Jews—killed only twelve hours before, perhaps a Diaspora Jew might have thought of asking whether taking Beirut was really necessary.

Time and time again, Menachem Begin and Yasir Arafat accuse each other of being the new Hitler. Neither is. But each is a terrorist, and a disgrace to his people. Except that Begin has infinitely superior power in his hands. Now, for the first time in history, a terrorist has the world's best armed forces at his disposal, for his own use. Yet, to employ it comfortably, he must raise the PLO's threats against the Israeli people to the category of a new Holocaust. Just as some partisans of the PLO need to elevate Israeli aggression against the Palestinian and Lebanese peoples to the equivalent of a new Holocaust.

The expressions of our Prime Minister in a letter to President Ronald Reagan, in which he asserts that he commanded an army at the gates of Berlin in 1945, amount to, in the best of cases, sheer stupidity. In the worst of cases, they are an insult to those who fought against the Nazi armies, which, even in defeat, were a thousand times more powerful than the PLO's guerrillas.

The assertion of Anthony Marlow, the Conservative British MP, at a demonstration on Trafalgar Square, that "a second Holocaust is in train of being carried out by the victims of the first," is an irresponsibility. An insult to the entire Jewish people.

The difference I find between Menachem Begin and all those throughout the world who now employ the same accusatory device is the sincerity of our Prime Minister. Menachem Begin is unbalanced, the others are mere hypocrites. Menachem Begin suffers from hallucinations, or, as Professor Zeev Mankowitz puts it, false analogies; the others center on opportunism.

Mankowitz, an authority on the Holocaust, writes:

"Is it really necessary to point out that Israel's hard-earned military power and carefully cultivated international standing give us a decisive edge over the Palestinians? The PLO has never been a match for Israeli arms and has never, in itself, posed a threat to Israel's survival. Indeed, the greater part of the Palestinian people are under direct Israeli control, while the remainder live under the shadow of Israeli military superiority. The intent of the PLO with regard to Israel—so clearly formulated in the Palestinian Covenant—must be exposed for what it is: a thinly disguised call to genocide. At the same time, this is not identical with the pseudoreligious commitment of the Nazis to murder every last Jew in the world."

Further on, he continues: "Are we really to view the miserable refugee camps as Munich and Nuremberg? Are we to understand that the flattened hovels outside of Sidon represent the Palestinian Dresden? Are we to see thousands of old people, women and children bereft of all and exposed to the elements as the paragons of a master race? Are we really to see Beirut as Berlin?

"There may be political method here, but it in no way detracts from the madness. Our Prime Minister is possessed of the unique ability of self-persuasion and, thereafter, his visceral vision becomes the guiding light of national policy. In transforming a justified punitive action and preventive measure into total war, without regard for the price to be exacted, Begin has lost touch with reality and is pursuing phantoms born in the greatest tragedy that ever befell our people.

"Whatever its final outcome, the epitaph to be placed upon the war in Lebanon will read: *Here lies the international stature and moral integrity of a wonderful people. Died of a false analogy.*"

Yes, we have killed our moral integrity. I feel that quite soon the Diaspora Jews will begin to experience the consequences of the process started by Menachem Begin, when they are denied the right to symbolize the pain of this century, the right to represent the universality of the victim. We are victims who have created our own victims in acts of cruelty. From now on, our tragedy will be inseparable from that of the Palestinians. Perhaps some of us will try to sidestep the Israeli moral collapse by resorting to statistics and comparing Auschwitz to Beirut. It will be in vain. The victims of Auschwitz would never have bombed Beirut. Our moral collapse cannot be diluted by statistics.

Abba Eban has perceived and described this descent into the darkness of a disguised Middle Ages. "There is," he writes, "a new vocabulary with special verbs: *to pound, to crush, to liquidate, to eradicate all to the last man, to cleanse, to fumigate, to solve by other means, not to put up with, to mean business, to wipe out.* It is hard to say what the effects of this lexicon will be as it resounds in an endless and squalid rhythm from one day to the next. Not one word of humility, compassion or restraint has come to the Israeli government in many weeks: nothing but the rhetoric of self-assertion, the hubris that the Greeks saw as the gravest danger to a man's fate.

"These weeks have been a dark age in the moral history of the Jewish people."

There will be many attempts to rewrite the history of these last two months. The Palestinians, however, should take care that the extremists, their terrorists, are not the ones who seize the facts. We Israelis must also take care that the writers are not those working for General Sharon. The task of the Palestinians will be easier, for they lived under the implacable iron hand of the Israeli Army. More difficult for us, who must remove the suffocating and false publicity campaign of our government so as to rework this operation of deceit, madness, and delusion which is cynically entitled "Peace for Galilee."

Palestinians and Israelis together must cut loose from the enormous mass of vested interests, from false geopolitical conceptions, from little anti-Semitic groups in search of justifications and pretexts, from little terrorist groups in search of money and jobs and weapons, from academics in search of new causes, and from Arab governments trying to avoid liberalizing their own countries.

In these past two months I have left behind many illusions, some fantasies, several obsessions. But none of my convictions.

Among all these things, there is one that shatters me beyond consolation. I have discovered in Jews a capacity for cruelty that I never believed possible.

Where do we go from here? To one more review of the blames and virtues accumulated in the last forty years? To using, in one sense or another (generally by falsifying history in favor of one or the other) the terrors and the crimes?

Yet it remains that survival is the most imperative problem of the Palestinians. I don't know how they will achieve it in the face of the paranoid way that Begin and Sharon employ Israeli military might to try to destroy them. Nevertheless, they will have to learn how on their own. They will have to survive without resorting to terrorism or violence. They will have to survive by using the huge moral capital yielded by their suffering in Lebanon at the hands of Israel. They will have to learn to survive on the bases of dignity and honor, on the message of the tragedy, on the morality of the victim— all of them attributes that before belonged to the Jews and now belong to the Palestinians.

And they will have to find leaders who will establish a political strategy that will defend their national identity and give them an independent nation.

We Israelis will do the same. We will defend our democracy. We will try to recover our dignity. We will try to rebuild our moral values. We will have to inspire the majority of Israelis to cherish democracy, to defeat the corruption of religious intolerance, to combat the obsession that tanks and planes represent our security, to recognize that Israel will have peace only when it can accept living together with a Palestinian state in the same region.

Despite all the blood, Palestinian and Israeli, which has been spilled on these lands in the nine weeks now ending, I believe that the time ahead will be very harsh, but surely less bloody. Perhaps even more cruel, but less homicidal.

It's certainly an obscenity on my part to refer in one breath to the Palestinian blood and to the Israeli blood spilled in Sharon's War. What happened to the Palestinians and the Lebanese in these months should neither be compared nor measured; it can stand by itself and be felt for itself.

In Israel, many people complain that this drama was exaggerated throughout the entire world. On the contrary, we should worry about its lack of impact. The Scandinavian peace militants who this summer went to the Soviet Union should have landed on Beirut's docks from thousands of small boats and ships. Amsterdam, New York, Rome, Paris, and London peace militants should have tried to break the Israeli Navy's blockade of Beirut, should have allowed their boats to be sunk by Israeli cannon. They should have proclaimed: "We're all Palestinians."

The peace movement has lost a historic opportunity.

During Juan Perón's second and third presidential terms, I saw Argentina seized by a collective madness, sometimes violent, sometimes peaceful; living in a mystical state, translating hallucinations into daily routine. There have been other countries in the past few years where I was able to witness such transports, which allow a government to manipulate collective terrors and impose an escape from reality through hallucination or messianism. This happened in Chile and Uruguay after 1972, and in Argentina after the military dictatorship took over in 1976.

I have relived this experience in Israel. Profound fears have been relived again because two men of enormous power are pursuing a messianic concept of geopolitics.

Here I have watched a repetition of the devices of complicity, involving presumably civilized people, just as in Argentina I saw politicians, lawyers, and journalists become accomplices in the greatest mass crime in Argentine history:

the kidnapping, torture, murder, and disappearance of more than fifteen thousand people. Here in Israel I have witnessed a complicity which is not portrayed as participation in a crime, but presented instead as sober analysis, as an explanation of a painful reality. An inclination to madness accomplished through the rationalization of a lesser evil. A soft silence. With the enchantment of a subtle silence.

The Palestinians will have to organize politically. They must do it on their own. Nobody will help them.

We Israelis will have to overcome our hallucinations through an effort of imagination, through an audacious ideological conception, through a total commitment to the struggle for democracy. A nation's madness usually ends in an explosion when the circumstances are ripe; it's what history shows. Perhaps we will be able to avoid this.

A first step toward our own salvation would be assuming responsibility for what we have done in Lebanon. I see no mechanism of conscience for the Israeli people other than the act of repairing what we have destroyed. It will be the quickest way to begin the reconstruction of our moral edifice and our democratic fabric.

To be sure, Begin will not want to do it. He will make announcements, appoint a committee, budget funds. But it will only be another exercise in philanthropy, in hypocrisy.

It is we, the Israelis, the people, who must do it. If today we are a minority, we're a minority by force of circumstances. And we will be a majority when our people discover that only we, the civilians, can guarantee peace, not Sharon's tanks and Begin's hallucinations.

We, and the Palestinian people, will rebuild Lebanon, not the Arab petrodollar millionaires nor the PLO's terrorists. Together we will also fashion a peaceful Palestinian country. And together we will also provide security to Israel. Not the omnipotence of our militarists.

While I think of how to finish these thoughts, I recall the Naked Emperor. It gladdens me to have been able to say that Begin is naked. During my adolescence, during my membership in a Zionist organization in Argentina, and, back in 1944, when I joined a farming settlement near Parana devoted to teaching Argentine Jews how to work the land, we considered Menachem Begin a terrorist who murdered indiscriminately, a Fascist. It gladdens me to have come to Israel to confirm it, and to be able to tell him that he is naked.

Derech Haifa, the highway to the north, runs in front of my house. Every morning at seven o'clock a truck or a bus brings the Arab workers from the villages near Tel Aviv where they are authorized to live. They are preparing the soil to plant a row of palms. My city has a good administrator who is filling it with flowers and trees. The Arab laborers toil, rest, pull out their water bottles, their meals, go back to work, and then get into the trucks or buses to return to their homes. They leave behind a touch of beauty. Each time they leave, my city is more beautiful. Looking at them from my balcony, I can only relieve myself by vomiting for this Israel which wants to be like South Africa. The heat is terrible; vomiting does me good. This is South Africa.

It will soon be three years that I have lived here. I have never been able to learn Hebrew. The first person who tried to teach me in Buenos Aires was, I think, my friend Jacobo Fridland, in 1938. Years later, he was killed by a Palestinian terrorist who infiltrated the Negev. We belonged to the same Zionist group. Since then I have tried many times but always failed. In a few weeks, come September, I'll try one more time. Three lessons a week—Tuesdays, Thursdays, and Sundays—five hours a day for six months. If I fail this time, I'll try to learn Arabic. For quite a long time, if we want to live in peace, understanding the other is going to be as necessary as understanding one's self. I remember a Polish film inspired by the devils of Loudon in which the exasperated rabbi finally tells the Catholic priest: "You are stupid if you don't understand me. I am you, and you are me." The same actor played both parts.

Sharon's War started Sunday, June 6, 1982. By Monday, June 7, the Israeli armored columns were already deep into

Lebanon. There was another Monday, June 7, thirty-four years ago.

On Monday, June 7, 1948, Jerusalem was left with hardly any food during the Arab siege in the War of Independence. Water was rationed and the stench of decomposing bodies was unbearable. The Arab Legion's shelling of our capital was inhuman, absurd, unnecessary. Jewish children died in the hospitals because of lack of water, food, medicines.

Two entire generations—not only in Israel but throughout the world—grew up with this image of a besieged, sacrificial Israel.

Today in Beirut Arab children have their legs and arms amputated by candlelight in the basements of hospitals destroyed by bombs, without anesthetics, without sterilization. It is eleven days since proud veteran Israeli troops cut the electricity and water, and food and fuel supplies. We're in August, a hot August. Rats already outnumber children in the city of Beirut, upon which the best pilots in the world, the aviators of the Israeli Air Force, are exercising their marvelous capacity for precision. From their planes they watch how the buildings of Beirut crumble. People in Beirut also observe those who leap from their windows, choosing a different death from those who were caught in buildings that were reduced to dust.

In the summer of 1948, there were those who left Jerusalem and those who stayed. The cowardly and the brave. There were doubts, mistakes, and recriminations. There were Jewish fighters and there were Jewish terrorists.

As in Beirut in the summer of 1982. Now history is Palestinian.

Yesterday ten Israeli soldiers who fell in the last attack against Beirut were buried with full military honors. The other nine will be buried today, Friday, August 6. In the same battle, 250 Palestinians and Lebanese, who will not have a burial for a while, also died; the rats will take care of a few. The 65 Israeli wounded are already being treated in the best field hospitals in the world—there are no hospitals for the 670

Palestinian and Lebanese wounded. It's possible that not all of them will perish from their wounds, and that some will survive the thirst.

Psalm 137 says I should never forget Jerusalem. I have never forgotten her. With the same fervor and tenderness, I will never forget Beirut.

Last night, demonstrators demanding peace and the total withdrawal of troops from Lebanon marched through the streets of Jerusalem bearing torches. The people of Jerusalem think of Beirut and struggle for Beirut. There is rage. There is hope.

Tel Aviv
August 8, 1982

The Massacre

On Sunday, September 19, 1982, the second day of the New Year, the second day of the month of Tishrei, 5743, there were no newspapers in Israel. Since the previous day, when the first stories about the massacre of Palestinians in Beirut had begun to circulate, the only reliable source for any kind of information had been the British Broadcasting Corporation out of London.

Twenty kilometers north of Tel Aviv, a group of youths from Kibbutz Gaash went out on the Haifa Highway and paralyzed all traffic. They barricaded the road with burning tires and stones. It was the first protest, spontaneous. What else could they do to express their indignation? It wasn't much, but they found it unbearable to remain indifferent. They cut the highway to the north that leads to Lebanon.

In Jerusalem, two or three hundred people took to the streets. They could not endure the idea of remaining in their homes, imagining scenes of what had occurred in Beirut. They talked, exchanged news, proclaimed their shame at being Israelis, and were clubbed and tear-gassed by police.

Along the Lebanese border, at Rosh Hanikra, a group of about a hundred protesters demonstrated. They were insulted and beaten by the majority of the Israelis at this popular tourist spot, and were dispersed by troops from the frontier garrison.

This is almost all that took place in Israel, even though news of the massacre of Palestinians had already been known for twenty-four hours, even though all of us realized it had been organized by our army.*

Why are the Israelis incapable of recognizing the high degree of criminality in their army's campaign against the Palestinian people?

As the killing in the camps started, at the very beginning, the bravest, ablest, and most honest of the Israeli war correspondents became aware of what was happening. Zeev Schiff reported his information to a member of the government, and begged him to intervene. And that was all.

He did not tell the international press, which would have tried to stop the killing. Israeli discipline prevailed in the journalist. For twenty years this discipline has intoxicated the Israeli people, and blackmailed Diaspora Jews. Israeli discipline led Schiff to deliver his information to one of those responsible for the massacre, a member of the Israeli cabinet.

Why was this able and honest reporter incapable of taking the measure of the high degree of criminality in the Israeli government?

On that Sunday, September 19, my oldest son came to say goodbye. He had been called to serve again, and was due to leave the following day for his base in the north. He had been there for the first forty days of the war. Now he has to return for another twenty. I believe he should not go, but the thought of military prison repels him. He is still traumatized by the memory of his visits to the jail in which I was imprisoned in Argentina. Yet, though he doesn't want to desert, he

*The following Saturday, September 25, there was a big rally in Tel Aviv, estimated by journalists here at more than 100,000 and inflated in the foreign press to an impossible 400,000, but the crowd was almost entirely composed of the ineffectual minority that has always opposed the Begin government. I believe that a majority of the people at the rally had been supporters of the invasion up to the time of the massacre.

does need to express in some way his protest against the killings in the Palestinian camps. He is majoring in the humanities at Tel Aviv University, and he is in love with anthropology. He questions me slowly and gently about life in prison.

Listen to the reply of an Israeli father, and reflect on the degree of abnormality, alienation, and deformity that has overtaken daily life in Israel:

"Son, you can't compare an Argentine jail to an Israeli jail. In our jails, only Arabs are maltreated, and you are a member of the superior race. It's true that once we were the people chosen by God to be witnesses of his truth, but now that we have girded ourselves for the murder of another people, we are a superior race since, as our government says, nobody can defeat us. They won't torture you in jail. Once you arrange your daily routine, thirty or sixty days pass quickly. But if you don't go now to your base, it will be merely an individual act. Perhaps others in your regiment think as you do, and together you can organize a collective protest. In any case, all of you must refuse to go to Lebanon. One can't be an accomplice in a crime and justify oneself by citing orders from above. It's time to rebel."

My son knows that Jews are not tortured in Israeli jails, but he also knows that conscientious objectors have to endure many humiliations. He left the next day, planning to speak with other soldiers.* I remembered Rabbi Robert Goldberg, who told young men who had refused to serve in the United States Army during the Vietnam War: "You may go to trial, but never to a future Nuremberg."

How is it possible that I can resign myself to leaving my son in the hands of the extremists who now command the Israeli Army?

I have little faith in Israel's democratic opposition. I fear that the Israeli discipline which totally dominates the sub-

---

*On October 4, 1982, Daniel Timerman was sentenced to twenty-eight days' confinement in a military prison for refusing to return to the Lebanese front.

conscious of all of us will result in an investigation that, in effect, protects the criminals from the punishment they deserve, and that the Israeli people will suffer an overwhelming loss of respect and moral standing in the eyes of the world. There have, after all, been many investigatory commissions over the years, but usually the reports are neither published nor acted upon. I remembered Rabbi Abraham Joshua Heschel, who declared during the campaign against the war in Vietnam: "In a free society, some are guilty but all are responsible."

Only the world's Jewish people, I believe, can now do something for us. The Diaspora Jews who have maintained the values of our moral and cultural traditions—those values now trampled on here by intolerance and Israeli nationalism —should establish a Jewish tribunal to pass judgment on Begin, Sharon, Eitan, and the entire general staff of the Israeli armed forces. This alone could be the means of working free of the sickness that is destroying Israel, and, perhaps, of preserving Israel's future.

What is it that has turned us into such efficient criminals?

I fear that in our collective subconscious, we may not be wholly repelled by the possibility of a Palestinian genocide. I don't believe we Israelis can be cured without the help of others.

Tel Aviv
September 21, 1982

A NOTE ABOUT THE AUTHOR

Jacobo Timerman was born in the Ukrainian town of Bar in 1923, and moved with his family to Argentina in 1928. A lifelong journalist, he founded two weekly newsmagazines in the 1960s and was a prominent news commentator on radio and television. He was the editor and publisher of the newspaper *La Opinión* from 1971 until his arrest by military authorities on April 15, 1977. Mr. Timerman now lives in Tel Aviv, Israel, with his wife and one of their three children.

A NOTE ON THE TYPE

The text of this book was set, via computer-driven cathode ray tube, in Caledonia, a typeface originally designed by W. A. Dwiggins. It belongs to the family of printing types called "modern faces" by printers—a term used to mark the change in style of type letters that occurred in about 1800. Caledonia borders on the general design of Scotch Modern, but is more freely drawn than that letter.

Composed, printed, and bound by
The Haddon Craftsmen, Inc.,
Scranton, Pennsylvania

Book design by Judith Henry